**ALEX** AND
**LAUREN LESTER**
founders of Cast Iron Keto

# CAST IRON KETO

### 75 Low-Carb One-Pot Meals for the Home Cook

PAGE STREET
PUBLISHING CO.

PAGE STREET
PUBLISHING CO.

First published in 2020 by

Page Street Publishing Co.

27 Congress Street, Suite 105

Salem, MA  01970

www.pagestreetpublishing.com

Distributed by Macmillan, sales in Canada by The Canadian Manda Group.

24   23   22   21   20      1   2   3   4   5

ISBN-13: 978-1-62414-984-9

ISBN-10: 1-62414-984-7

Library of Congress Control Number:  2019943011

Cover and book design by Laura Benton for Page Street Publishing Co.

Photography by Lauren Lester

Printed and bound in the United States

# CONTENTS

# S

## BRILLIANT BOWLS 115

## SENSATIONAL SALADS 135

## MEATLESS MONDAYS: VEGETARIAN 153

# INTRODUCTION
## OUR STORY

### Alex

Hey there! I'm Alex, and I'm so excited that you picked up our book! After I made my favorite post-workout breakfast hash in my go-to cast iron skillet, I thought, "We should start a blog called Cast Iron Keto." Lauren took the idea and ran with it. Within twenty-four hours, the website was built and we had a list of twenty recipes to launch with. We knew we had an awesome idea that could help others make delicious Keto food while saving time and money by using the one-pot method. I mean, what's easier than one-pot dishes? After launching Cast Iron Keto in 2017, we quickly realized that our readers love this concept just as much as we do.

My background in Keto started with the desire to live an epic life. For me, this means fueling my body in a way that allows me to be active. I grew up as a Boy Scout and Eagle Scout, and a love for the outdoors was ingrained in me from the start. However, my story goes like most. Once I went to college, I became overweight and unhappy and found my meals consisting of Cheetos, pizza, and Japanese takeout. I then met my lovely wife, Lauren, who was in the same boat. We decided to shape up our diet and, in turn, I shaped up too.

Now my days are spent running, biking, swimming, hiking, and traveling. Functional exercise is what I love most. To fuel these adventures, I've found my happy spot with a Keto-style diet that is low in carbs, high in fat, and moderate in protein. Cast Iron Keto isn't an "eat a 48-ounce (1.3-kg) rib eye with bacon on the side for dinner" website and neither is this book. We focus on whole foods—tons of plants; high-quality, grass-fed, pastured, or wild-caught proteins; and healthy fats. I'm excited for you to dive into these recipes and make this book a go-to resource in your kitchen.

### Lauren

Hi, I'm Lauren! I have a passion for cooking and, of course, eating. Ever since I was little, food has been my hobby. I'm the type of person who will think about lunch before I'm done with breakfast. Seriously, I love food. I've taken that passion and harnessed it into a creative business of recipe development, food photography, and food styling.

In 2012, I founded the popular Paleo food blog Wicked Spatula after switching to a gluten-free diet to help treat various autoimmune diseases. Through exploring Paleo cooking, my love affair with allergen-friendly (and, eventually, Keto-friendly) recipes was born. Healthful Creative, our food media company, was founded in 2016, and Cast Iron Keto followed shortly thereafter. While we sold Wicked Spatula in 2019, I'm forever grateful for its audience, who believed in me and set the foundation for my career.

I've found great relief in the Keto way of eating for my autoimmune issues, just like I did when I initially went Paleo in 2012. I believe that food is medicine. I also believe that there should be no sacrifice in flavor when cooking healthy, low-carb, and gluten-free dishes. Long gone are the days of bland boiled chicken and broccoli. If you're new to this way of eating, I want to inspire you to create food that will not only taste great but also fuel your mind and body to their fullest potential. And if you're a Keto veteran, I hope you find new favorite recipes to add to your arsenal.

*Alex Lester*

*Lauren Lester*

# RECIPE ICON KEY

| | | | |
|---|---|---|---|
| | Dairy-Free | | Nut-Free |
| | Egg-Free | | Soy-Free |
| | Gluten-Free | 30 | Whole 30 |

# WHY CAST IRON?

I think the better question is, *why not cast iron*? A well-seasoned cast iron pan is as irreplaceable in the kitchen as a sharp knife or a hot oven, and here are our top three reasons why.

### Reason 1: Cast Iron Skillets Are the Swiss Army Knives of the Kitchen
You can use a cast iron skillet in the oven, on the stove, or over a campfire. You can use one to roast a chicken or bake a cake. If you're in a pinch and can't find a meat mallet, well, you can use your imagination on that one. A good cast iron skillet is one of the most utilitarian kitchen tools imaginable and no kitchen is complete without at least one. It can replace so many single-function kitchen tools and gadgets and can inadvertently declutter your kitchen. Since our skillet serves so many purposes, we often refer to it as the Swiss Army knife of the kitchen.

### Reason 2: It's an Investment
A good cast iron skillet is one of the only things you can buy these days that you'll likely never have to worry about replacing. They are practically indestructible and they aren't subject to the same level of wear and tear as nonstick skillets; in fact, the more you cook with a cast iron skillet or Dutch oven, the more seasoned it becomes and, like a fine wine, it just gets better with age. With routine care, your cast iron cookware could become a cherished family heirloom to be passed down throughout generations.

### Reason 3: It's Nontoxic
Maybe you've picked up this book to try the Ketogenic diet for the first time, or maybe you are already a Keto veteran who is on the lookout for delicious low-carb, high-fat recipes. Regardless, you've picked this book up because you care about your health. Cast iron cookware is one of the healthiest ways to prepare your meals and has been used for generations. Unlike nonstick cookware, cast iron contains no harmful chemicals like PFOA, making cast iron the perfect choice for a health-minded kitchen.

# HOW TO CARE FOR CAST IRON

Here are the steps you need to follow to season cast iron:

- If it's a brand-new skillet, wash it with warm, soapy water. This is the only time you need to wash your skillet with soap; from now on, hot water and maybe a pinch of coarse salt should do the trick.

- If it's an old skillet that hasn't been used in a while or needs a periodic reseasoning (every six months), scrub away any rust or stuck-on food. This may require steel wool or another type of abrasive pad, such as a chain-mail scrubber.

- Preheat the oven to 200°F (93°C). Thoroughly dry the skillet and place it in the oven for 10 minutes.

- Remove the warm skillet from the oven and turn the heat up to 450°F (232°C). Use a clean rag or paper towel to apply a thin layer of flax oil all over the skillet.

- Allow the oil to soak into the iron and wipe away the excess. (If you don't wipe it all away, it's going to fill your kitchen with lots of smoke and leave a sticky residue on the skillet.)

- Place the skillet upside down in the oven for 1 hour.

- After the hour is up, pull the skillet out of the oven and allow it to cool for 5 to 10 minutes on the stove or another heat-safe surface. Then repeat this process two or three more times, until you are satisfied with the result. These directions also work for cast iron Dutch ovens, though there is no need to season ceramic-coated cast iron.

Here are the steps for daily care of your cast iron:

- After cooking with your skillet, simply wipe it out with a rag and hot water.

- If there's stuck-on food, you can use a coarse salt or a chain-mail scrubber to help remove it. After washing the skillet, dry it completely.

- If the skillet is dry and dull, wipe it down with a very thin layer of flax oil, making sure to remove the excess. There's no need to bake it as you would when seasoning unless the skillet is very dry and in need of reseasoning.

- Store your skillet in a dry place.

# THE BASICS OF KETO

The Ketogenic diet is a high-fat, moderate-protein, low-carb approach to losing weight and is also used to enhance physical performance and treat diseases from epilepsy to diabetes. To reap all the amazing benefits of the Keto diet, you'll need to follow a low-carb approach where 5 to 10 percent of your daily calories come from carbohydrates, about 25 percent come from protein, and the remaining amount comes from healthy fat sources.

When your body enters a state of nutritional ketosis, you stop relying on glucose as fuel and start relying on fat to fuel your body.

If you've ever had low blood sugar and been hangry, that is a side effect of relying on glucose, as it is a less efficient fuel source than fat. Alex can attest that when he would go for long runs while eating a high-carb diet, he would have to carry some sort of sugary gel or goo to keep him going. After adopting a Keto diet, Alex has all the fuel he needs stored in his body, ready to burn. This fat burning leads to effortless weight loss for many.

## But I Thought Fat Was Bad . . .

We think Michael Pollan said it best: "Nutrition science is kind of where surgery was in the year 1650, which is to say very interesting and promising, but do you really want to get on the table yet?"

For so long, fat was the enemy—everything we were told (or sold) promoted a low-fat diet. The unintended consequence of removing dietary fat from our food supply was that it had to be replaced by something to maintain food's caloric value.

Unfortunately, all too often that fat was replaced with cereal grains or sugar. We, as a society, are moving away from the dietary guidelines that vilified fat and glorified grains. There is a huge difference between what we call the fat that hangs around our midsection (adipose tissue) and the dietary fat that is a vital macronutrient and energy source.

The Keto diet is a tremendous paradigm shift from what we've always been told about eating healthy, and until recently it's been somewhat on the fringe of nutritional science. New studies showing the benefits of this way of eating are being released on a weekly, if not daily, basis showing the Keto diet's effectiveness in treating diseases, promoting weight loss, and improving overall health.

## Is the Keto Diet Right for Me?

Maybe—we can't tell you that. Each and every person on this planet is different, so it stands to reason there is no singular diet for all. What we can tell you is that the Ketogenic diet has had a huge impact on our lives, and we encourage anyone looking to lose weight or treat an ailment to check it out. There are many different approaches to eating a Ketogenic diet: the standard Ketogenic diet, the targeted Ketogenic diet, and the cyclical Ketogenic diet. Which one is right for you depends on your goals—it's not "one size fits all."

# LAND

Dishes like Crispy Sesame Chicken (page 40), Italian Sub Sandwich Casserole (page 32), and Blue Cheese and Pecan–Stuffed Pork Tenderloin (page 47) are sure to liven up your dinner table. Keto recipes are sometimes thought to be just meat and cheese with not a vegetable in sight, but we're changing things up with delicious meat dishes that are also veggie-packed to fuel your body, mind, and taste buds.

**SERVES 4**

**NUTRITION**

(per serving)

**Calories**
388 kcal

**Fat**
27.1 g

**Protein**
28.1 g

**Carbs**
8.5 g

**Fiber**
2.4 g

**Net Carbs**
6.1 g

# CHICKEN PUTTANESCA

One of Lauren's favorite dishes to make has always been fresh puttanesca sauce. The briny anchovies, crushed tomatoes, and salty olives hit the spot. To give this classic dish a twist, we're spinning it into a quick and easy skillet dinner using chicken as the protein. Feel free to swap seared scallops or mussels for the chicken, as seafood pairs equally well with the sauce.

¼ cup (60 ml) plus 2 tbsp (30 ml) olive oil, divided

1 lb (454 g) chicken fillets

1 tsp sea salt, divided

½ tsp black pepper, divided

½ cup (80 g) diced white onion

3 cloves garlic, minced

1 tbsp (3 g) Italian seasoning

½ tsp red pepper flakes

3 anchovy fillets, minced

1½ cups (182 g) crushed tomatoes

Juice of 1 lemon

½ cup (50 g) Kalamata olives

¼ cup (15 g) minced fresh parsley

Heat 2 tablespoons (30 ml) of the oil in a 10-inch (25-cm) or larger cast iron skillet over medium-high heat. Season the chicken with ½ teaspoon of the salt and ¼ teaspoon of the black pepper. Sear the chicken for 3 to 4 minutes per side, until it is golden and the internal temperature reaches 165°F (74°C). Transfer the chicken to a plate and set it aside.

Add the remaining ¼ cup (60 ml) oil to the skillet and reduce the heat to medium. Once the oil is hot, add the onion and garlic. Cook for 4 to 5 minutes, until the onion is soft but not brown. Add the Italian seasoning, red pepper flakes, remaining ½ teaspoon of salt, remaining ¼ teaspoon of black pepper, and anchovy fillets. Cook the mixture for 1 minute, until it is fragrant.

Add the crushed tomatoes and lemon juice. Bring the sauce to a simmer and cook for 5 minutes. Return the chicken to the skillet and add the olives and parsley. Cook for 3 to 4 minutes, until the chicken is warm. Serve immediately.

# PESTO AND ITALIAN SAUSAGE SKILLET

A spin-off of one of our most popular recipes on our blog, this Pesto and Italian Sausage Skillet is packed with flavor. Feel free to make your own pesto, or use a store-bought variety to save a bit of time.

**SERVES 6**

**NUTRITION**

(per serving)

**Calories**
519 kcal

**Fat**
46.2 g

**Protein**
19 g

**Carbs**
8.2 g

**Fiber**
2.3 g

**Net Carbs**
5.9 g

### Nut Free Pesto

1 cup (71 g) packed fresh basil leaves

1 clove garlic

½ cup (120 ml) olive oil

¼ cup (25 g) grated Parmesan cheese

### Italian Sausage Skillet

2 tbsp (30 ml) olive oil

6 Italian sausages, sliced into 1-inch (2.5-cm) pieces

1 small head cabbage, cut into 1-inch (2.5-cm) thick slices

4 medium Roma tomatoes, seeded and diced

4 oz (112 g) shredded mozzarella cheese

Preheat the broiler to 500°F (260°C).

To make the pesto, combine the basil and garlic in a food processor and pulse until they are minced. With the processor running, slowly drizzle in the oil. Stir in the Parmesan cheese.

To make the Italian sausage skillet, heat the oil in a 10-inch (25-cm) or larger cast iron skillet over medium-high heat. Add the sausages and brown them for 2 to 3 minutes per side.

Cover the sausages with the cabbage, cover the skillet, and cook the mixture for 3 minutes. Uncover the skillet and stir in the tomatoes. Cook for 3 minutes, until the cabbage is wilted. Stir in 6 tablespoons (96 g) of the pesto and top the mixture with the mozzarella.

Transfer the skillet to the oven and broil for 4 to 5 minutes, until the cheese is bubbly. Serve immediately.

Store the remaining pesto in a glass jar or container in the refrigerator for up to one week. Pesto may also be frozen for up to one year.

## SERVES 4

## NUTRITION

(per serving)

**Calories**
570 kcal

**Fat**
43.1 g

**Protein**
32.2 g

**Carbs**
12.5 g

**Fiber**
3.8 g

**Net Carbs**
8.7 g

# CLASSIC INDIAN CHICKEN CURRY

A few years ago, we fell in love with a little local curry shop and have since been infatuated with Indian food. The heavily spiced, aromatic dishes are comforting and packed with flavor. We like to serve this dish with cauliflower rice, sliced serrano peppers, and maybe some cucumber for extra crunch.

### Curry
1 small onion

2 medium serrano peppers

1 (1-inch [2.5-cm]) piece fresh ginger, peeled

2 cloves garlic

½ cup (8 g) fresh cilantro leaves and stems

2 tbsp (30 ml) water

¼ cup (55 g) ghee

2 tsp (6 g) ground turmeric

1½ tsp (5 g) ground cumin

1 tsp ground coriander

1 tsp garam masala

2 tbsp (30 g) tomato paste

1¼ lbs (568 g) boneless, skinless chicken thighs, diced

1 cup (240 ml) heavy cream

Sea salt, as needed

4 cups (480 g) cooked cauliflower rice

### Toppings
1 medium serrano pepper, thinly sliced

¼ cup (15 g) minced fresh cilantro

To make the curry, combine the onion, serrano peppers, ginger, garlic, cilantro, and water in a food processor and process until the ingredients are smooth.

Melt the ghee in a 10-inch (25-cm) or larger cast iron skillet over medium-high heat. Add the onion mixture and sauté for 5 minutes, until it is fragrant.

Add the turmeric, cumin, coriander, and garam masala and cook the mixture for 30 seconds, until it is fragrant.

Add the tomato paste and stir to combine. Add the chicken and reduce the heat to medium.

Simmer the curry for 10 minutes, then stir in the cream. Cover the skillet and simmer for 20 minutes. Taste the curry for salt and adjust the seasoning if needed. Top the curry with the serrano pepper and cilantro and serve it with the cauliflower rice.

# CRISPY PORK BELLY
## WITH KIMCHI COLLARD GREENS

If you've never tried pork belly, think of it as very thick slices of bacon. Sounds good, right? We've paired it with spicy kimchi and earthy collard greens to create the perfect flavor explosion. Because we grew up in the South, collard greens are one of our favorite vegetables, but we like to put a fun spin on things—that's where the kimchi comes in!

**SERVES 4**

**NUTRITION**

(per serving)

**Calories**
635 kcal

**Fat**
60.9 g

**Protein**
14.7 g

**Carbs**
7.7 g

**Fiber**
5.3 g

**Net Carbs**
2.4 g

1 lb (454 g) pork belly

Sea salt, as needed

Black pepper, as needed

1 large bunch collard greens

1 clove garlic, minced

2 tbsp (30 ml) apple cider vinegar

½ cup (70 g) kimchi

Preheat the oven to 425°F (218°C). Slice a crisscross pattern into the top layer of fat on the pork belly. Season the pork liberally with the salt and black pepper and place it in a 10-inch (25-cm) or larger cast iron skillet.

Bake the pork for 35 minutes. Reduce the heat to 325°F (163°C) and bake for 30 more minutes, until the top of the pork is crispy and golden. If needed, broil the pork for 4 to 5 minutes at the end of the cooking time to make sure the top is very crispy.

Remove the pork from the oven and let it rest for 15 minutes before slicing.

While the pork is resting, drain out all but 3 tablespoons (45 ml) of the fat in the skillet and place the skillet over medium-high heat. Working in batches, add the collard greens, garlic, and vinegar to the skillet. Cook the collards for 7 to 10 minutes, until they are very wilted. Turn off the heat and stir in the kimchi.

To serve, slice the pork belly and serve the slices with the collard greens.

## SERVES 4

## NUTRITION
(per serving)

**Calories**
460 kcal

**Fat**
30.2 g

**Protein**
37.1 g

**Carbs**
11.2 g

**Fiber**
4.4 g

**Net Carbs**
6.8 g

# ARROZ CON POLLO

Crispy chicken thighs, fragrant cauliflower rice, and briny olives complete this skillet dinner. We use bone-in, skin-on chicken thighs for the flavor factor, but you could also use boneless chicken thighs as well. Just be sure to adjust the cooking time accordingly.

1 tsp ground coriander

1 tsp ground cumin

1 tsp sea salt

½ tsp garlic powder

1 tsp dried oregano

¼ tsp black pepper

4 (6-oz [168-g]) bone-in, skin-on chicken thighs

¼ cup (60 ml) plus 2 tbsp (30 ml) avocado oil, divided

1 small bell pepper (any color), diced

½ cup (80 g) diced white onion

2 cloves garlic, minced

¼ cup (60 ml) chicken broth

¼ cup (30 g) crushed tomatoes

12 oz (336 g) uncooked cauliflower rice

8 large pimento-stuffed green olives

2 tbsp (8 g) minced fresh cilantro

In a small bowl, mix together the coriander, cumin, salt, garlic powder, oregano, and black pepper. Season the chicken with the spice mixture. Set the chicken aside.

Heat 2 tablespoons (30 ml) of the oil in a 10-inch (25-cm) or larger cast iron skillet over high heat. Add the chicken, skin side down, and sear it for 5 to 6 minutes without moving it. Flip the chicken and cook for 10 to 15 minutes, until the chicken's internal temperature reaches 165°F (74°C). Transfer the chicken to a plate.

Add the remaining ¼ cup (60 ml) of oil, bell pepper, onion, and garlic to the skillet. Cook, stirring, for 5 to 6 minutes, until the vegetables have softened. Add the broth and crushed tomatoes.

Bring the mixture to a simmer, then add in the cauliflower rice. Cook for 4 to 5 minutes, until the cauliflower rice is fluffy. Transfer the chicken and any accumulated juices back to the skillet. Cook for 1 to 2 minutes to reheat the chicken.

Top the arroz con pollo with the olives and cilantro and serve.

# CHIPOTLE CHICKEN STEW

Avocado and Cotija cheese are the Keto equivalents of a cherry on top of this stew. Everyone gathered around the table will be excited for this dinner. Don't be surprised if even the pickiest eaters are asking for a second bowl—pretty please, with Cotija on top.

**SERVES 4**

## NUTRITION
(per serving)

**Calories**
643 kcal

**Fat**
56.7 g

**Protein**
20.5 g

**Carbs**
14.5 g

**Fiber**
7.1 g

**Net Carbs**
7.5 g

### Stew
¼ cup (60 ml) avocado oil

1 medium onion, coarsely chopped

2 cloves garlic, minced

1 tbsp (7 g) paprika

2 tsp (6 g) ground cumin

½ tsp dried oregano

½ tsp sea salt

1 lb (454 g) boneless, skinless chicken thighs, cut into 2-inch (5-cm) pieces

1 (15-oz [420-g]) can diced fire-roasted tomatoes with green chiles, drained

1 cup (240 ml) chicken broth

3 tbsp (45 ml) pureed chipotle peppers in adobo sauce

### Toppings
¼ cup (31 g) crumbled Cotija cheese

1 medium avocado, diced

¼ cup (15 g) minced fresh cilantro

4 medium radishes, thinly sliced

To make the stew, heat the oil in a 5-quart (4.8-L) cast iron Dutch oven over medium heat. Add the onion and garlic and sauté them for 3 to 4 minutes, until the onion is starting to soften. Add the paprika, cumin, oregano, and salt and cook 30 seconds, until the mixture is fragrant.

Add the chicken and brown it for 3 minutes per side. Add the tomatoes, broth, and chipotle peppers to the pot. Stir to combine.

Reduce the heat to medium-low, bring the stew to a gentle simmer, cover the Dutch oven, and cook the stew for 30 minutes.

To serve, divide the stew among 4 bowls and top the stew with the Cotija cheese, avocado, cilantro, and radishes.

# CHICKEN SCHNITZEL

**Crispy chicken plus tangy sauerkraut create a perfect German-inspired dinner. We love using pork rinds as the breading—they make an incredibly crunchy crust and fry to a perfect golden brown.**

## SERVES 4

## NUTRITION

(per serving)

**Calories**
794 kcal

**Fat**
66 g

**Protein**
42.4 g

**Carbs**
4.2 g

**Fiber**
1.8 g

**Net Carbs**
2.4 g

1 large egg

1 tbsp (15 ml) heavy cream

¾ cup (75 g) shredded Parmesan cheese

½ cup (53 g) pork rind crumbs

1 tbsp (3 g) Italian seasoning

1 cup (240 ml) avocado or algae oil

4 (4-oz [112-g]) chicken cutlets

1 cup (142 g) sauerkraut

1 medium lemon, quartered

1 tbsp (4 g) minced parsley

In a shallow bowl, beat the egg and cream together. On a medium plate, combine the Parmesan cheese, pork rind crumbs, and Italian seasoning.

Heat the oil in a 10-inch (25-cm) or larger skillet over medium-high heat. Dip each cutlet into the egg then dredge it through the cheese mixture. Carefully place the cutlet into the oil and fry it for 3 to 4 minutes per side, until it is golden brown and the internal temperature reaches 165°F (74°C).

Serve the schnitzel with the sauerkraut, lemon, and parsley.

# BRUSCHETTA CHICKEN

A great way to use up juicy tomatoes and fresh basil, this Bruschetta Chicken is the perfect summertime patio kind of meal.

**NUTRITION**

(per serving)

**Calories**
559 kcal

**Fat**
41.7 g

**Protein**
35.5 g

**Carbs**
11 g

**Fiber**
4.9 g

**Net Carbs**
6.1 g

### Bruschetta
2 medium tomatoes, diced

2 cloves garlic, minced

¼ cup (38 g) coarsely chopped red onion

2 tbsp (10 g) minced fresh basil

1 tbsp (15 ml) olive oil

1 tbsp (15 ml) balsamic vinegar

Sea salt, as needed

Black pepper, as needed

### Chicken
2 (8-oz [224-g]) chicken breasts, pounded to 1-inch (2.5-cm) thick

¼ tsp sea salt

1 tsp Italian seasoning

3 tbsp (45 ml) olive oil

4 (1-oz [28-g]) slices fresh mozzarella cheese

### Arugula Salad
4 cups (40 g) arugula

¼ cup (25 g) shaved Parmesan cheese

1 medium avocado, diced

1 tbsp (7 g) finely chopped preserved lemon

3 tbsp (45 ml) olive oil

Sea salt, as needed

Black pepper, as needed

To make the bruschetta, combine the tomatoes, garlic, onion, basil, oil, vinegar, salt, and black pepper in a medium bowl. Set the bruschetta aside until ready to serve.

To make the chicken, season the chicken with the salt and Italian seasoning. Heat the oil in a 10-inch (25-cm) or larger cast iron skillet over medium heat.

Add the chicken to the skillet and cook it for 6 to 7 minutes per side, until it is brown and its internal temperature reaches 165°F (74°C).

Top each chicken breast with the mozzarella cheese and cover the skillet to allow the cheese to melt slightly. Cut the breasts in half and top them with the bruschetta.

To make the arugula salad, combine the arugula, Parmesan cheese, avocado, lemon, oil, salt, and black pepper in a large bowl. Toss the salad and serve it alongside the chicken.

## SERVES 4

## NUTRITION
(per serving)

**Calories**
635 kcal

**Fat**
50 g

**Protein**
38.4 g

**Carbs**
7.8 g

**Fiber**
2.1 g

**Net Carbs**
5.8 g

# CHEESEBURGER-STUFFED MUSHROOM CAPS

**We're swapping out the buns for portobello caps and we're never looking back. These caps create the perfect vessel for cheesy beef plus all the toppings you'd expect on your favorite cheeseburger.**

### Mushroom Caps
4 (3-oz [84-g]) portobello caps

1 tbsp (15 ml) avocado oil

4 slices bacon, coarsely chopped

1 lb (454 g) ground beef

2 cups (226 g) shredded Cheddar cheese

1 tsp garlic salt

¼ cup (40 g) minced onion

¼ cup (39 g) diced dill pickles

¼ cup (39 g) diced tomatoes

### Toppings
½ cup (24 g) shredded lettuce

1 tbsp (16 g) yellow mustard

4 dill pickle chips

To make the mushroom caps, preheat the oven to 450°F (232°C).

Remove the middle of the mushroom caps and use them for another recipe. Toss the caps with the oil and set them aside.

Heat a 10-inch (25-cm) or larger cast iron skillet over medium-high heat. Add the bacon to the skillet and cook for 3 to 4 minutes, until it is crispy. Remove the bacon and set it aside, leaving the grease in the skillet.

Add the beef to the skillet and cook until it is browned, about 7 minutes. Add the bacon to the skillet and stir to combine. Transfer the beef mixture to a large bowl and add the Cheddar cheese, garlic salt, onion, pickles, and tomatoes.

Divide the mixture between the portobello caps. Place the caps in the skillet and transfer it to the oven to bake for about 10 minutes, until the cheese is melted.

Top each mushroom cap with the lettuce, mustard, and a pickle chip before serving.

# REUBEN CASSEROLE

This casserole—with its layers of corned beef, cheese, Thousand Island dressing, and sauerkraut—will satisfy even the most ferocious Reuben sandwich craving. Be sure to look for a sugar-free Thousand Island dressing (we like Primal Kitchen brand).

3 cups (426 g) sauerkraut, drained and squeezed dry

3 medium Roma tomatoes, seeded and cut into quarters

½ cup (120 ml) sugar-free Thousand Island dressing

12 oz (336 g) deli-sliced corned beef, coarsely chopped

2 cups (216 g) shredded Swiss cheese

2 tbsp (8 g) minced fresh parsley

Preheat the oven to 400°F (204°C).

Place the sauerkraut in the bottom of a 10-inch (25-cm) or larger cast iron skillet. Top it with the tomatoes, Thousand Island dressing, corned beef, and Swiss cheese.

Bake the casserole for 25 minutes, until the cheese is bubbly. Garnish the casserole with the parsley and serve.

**SERVES 6**

**NUTRITION**

(per serving)

**Calories**
369 kcal

**Fat**
29 g

**Protein**
21.1 g

**Carbs**
6.4 g

**Fiber**
2.7 g

**Net Carbs**
3.7 g

# ITALIAN SUB SANDWICH CASSEROLE

This casserole is what happens when a pot pie marries into the Mafia. All joking aside, this Italian Sub Sandwich Casserole has all of the classic sub sandwich flavors. It's delicious hot or cold, so it is great for leftovers.

**SERVES 6**

**NUTRITION**

(per serving)

**Calories**
581 kcal

**Fat**
44.3 g

**Protein**
35.9 g

**Carbs**
10.4 g

**Fiber**
3.2 g

**Net Carbs**
7.2 g

## Crust

1½ cups (170 g) part-skim, low-moisture shredded mozzarella cheese

⅔ cup (66 g) almond flour

2 large egg whites

1 tsp xanthan gum (optional)

## Filling

8 oz (224 g) sugar-free sliced deli ham

8 slices salami

8 slices pepperoni

8 slices capicola

8 slices provolone cheese, divided

1 medium bell pepper (any color), thinly sliced

2 medium Roma tomatoes, diced

1 cup (100 g) pitted black or Kalamata olives

¼ medium red onion, thinly sliced

½ cup (113 g) pickled banana peppers

2 tbsp (30 ml) olive oil

1 tbsp (15 ml) red wine vinegar

1 tbsp (3 g) Italian seasoning

Preheat the oven to 400°F (204°C).

To make the crust, put the mozzarella cheese in a medium microwave-safe bowl and microwave it just until it has melted, about 30 seconds.

Add the flour, egg whites, and xanthan gum (if using) to the cheese, stirring to combine.

Roll the dough into a ball and knead it 1 or 2 times. Place the dough between 2 sheets of parchment paper. Using a rolling pin, roll the dough out to a 10½-inch (27-cm) circle that is about ½ inch (13 mm) thick.

To make the filling, layer the remaining ingredients into a 10-inch (25-cm) or larger cast iron skillet in this order: ham, salami, pepperoni, capicola, 4 slices of the provolone cheese, bell pepper, tomatoes, olives, onion, and banana peppers.

Top the filling with the oil, vinegar, Italian seasoning, remaining 4 slices of provolone cheese, and the prepared crust.

Bake the casserole for 25 to 30 minutes, until the crust is browned. Serve the casserole immediately.

# PHILLY CHEESESTEAK SKILLET

Who doesn't love a good Philly cheesesteak? Tender steak with sautéed peppers, onions, and mushrooms plus melty cheese makes for one awesome dinner. If you're the type who likes marinara with your cheesesteak, feel free to add some to the skillet or serve it on the side.

1 lb (454 g) rib eye steak, thinly sliced

1 tsp sea salt, plus more as needed

¼ cup (56 g) unsalted butter

4 oz (112 g) button mushrooms, halved

1 medium bell pepper (any color), thinly sliced

½ large white onion, thinly sliced

1½ cups (170 g) shredded provolone cheese

Season the steak with the salt.

Heat a 10-inch (25-cm) or larger cast iron skillet over medium-high heat. Add the butter to the skillet and allow it to melt. Add the steak and sear it for 5 to 6 minutes. Add the mushrooms and cook them for 3 minutes, then add the bell pepper and onion.

Cook the steak mixture for about 5 minutes, until the pepper and onion are soft. Season the mixture with salt as needed. Sprinkle the provolone cheese over the top of the steak mixture. Cover the skillet and cook for 3 to 4 minutes to allow the cheese to melt. Serve the cheesesteak immediately.

## SERVES 4

### NUTRITION
(per serving)

**Calories**
562 kcal

**Fat**
45.5 g

**Protein**
33.8 g

**Carbs**
5.5 g

**Fiber**
1.3 g

**Net Carbs**
4.2 g

## SERVES 6

## NUTRITION

(per serving)

**Calories**
371 kcal

**Fat**
26.2 g

**Protein**
20.3 g

**Carbs**
13.8 g

**Fiber**
5.1 g

**Net Carbs**
8.7 g

# CLASSIC STUFFED PEPPERS

These Keto-friendly stuffed peppers are the ultimate weeknight dinner with their quick prep, even quicker cleanup, and deliciousness to top it off. This recipe is for a traditional stuffed pepper with ground beef, tomato, garlic, onion, and spices topped with melted cheese. Sometimes you don't mess with the classics.

2 tbsp (30 ml) avocado oil

1 lb (454 g) ground beef

1 tsp dried oregano

1 tsp paprika

1 tsp sea salt

¼ tsp black pepper

1 medium onion, coarsely chopped

3 cloves garlic, minced

1 tbsp (15 g) tomato paste

1 (15-oz [420-g]) can diced tomatoes, drained

1½ cups (180 g) uncooked cauliflower rice

6 medium bell peppers (any color), tops and cores removed

1 cup (113 g) shredded Monterey Jack cheese

2 tbsp (8 g) finely chopped fresh parsley

Preheat the oven to 400°F (204°C).

Heat the oil in a 10-inch (25-cm) or larger cast iron skillet over medium-high heat. Add the beef, oregano, paprika, salt, and black pepper and brown the beef for 5 to 7 minutes. Add the onion and garlic. Cook the mixture for 4 to 5 minutes.

Add the tomato paste, diced tomatoes, and cauliflower rice to the skillet. Cook for 5 minutes, then divide the mixture among the bell peppers and top them with the Monterey Jack cheese. Wipe out the skillet, then place the filled peppers in the skillet, cover the skillet with foil, and bake the peppers for 30 minutes. Uncover the skillet and bake the peppers for 10 minutes more, until the cheese is bubbly.

Top the peppers with the parsley and serve.

# CHEESY ROTISSERIE CHICKEN CASSEROLE

We love the hack of using a rotisserie chicken, because it means that dinner comes together in a flash. Can we talk about the green chile sauce for a second? It's delicious—like, lick-the-spoon delicious. Pro tip: Use fresh roasted green chiles if you can find them.

## Sauce
12-oz (336-g) can diced green chiles, undrained
½ cup (96 g) sour cream
2 tbsp (30 ml) avocado oil
Juice of 1 large lime
2 cloves garlic
½ cup (8 g) packed fresh cilantro leaves
Sea salt, as needed

## Filling
3 cups (360 g) uncooked cauliflower rice
1 (1¼-lb [568-g]) rotisserie chicken, pulled
1 (10-oz [280-g]) can Rotel Original, drained
1 tsp ground cumin
1 tsp gluten-free taco seasoning
½ tsp sea salt
2 cups (226 g) shredded Mexican blend cheese

## Toppings
¼ cup (48 g) sour cream
2 medium jalapeño peppers, thinly sliced
2 medium avocados, diced
4 medium radishes, thinly sliced
2 tbsp (8 g) minced cilantro

Preheat the oven to 400°F (204°C).

To make the sauce, combine the green chiles, sour cream, oil, lime juice, garlic, cilantro, and salt in a food processor. Process the ingredients until they are smooth.

To make the filling, place the cauliflower rice in the bottom of a 10-inch (25-cm) or larger cast iron skillet. Top the cauliflower rice with the chicken, Rotel, and the green chile sauce. Sprinkle the top of the filling with the cumin, taco seasoning, and salt. Stir to combine.

Top the casserole with the Mexican blend cheese and bake for 15 to 20 minutes, until the cheese is bubbly.

Top the casserole with the sour cream, jalapeño peppers, avocados, radishes, and cilantro and serve.

# CRISPY SESAME CHICKEN

**Lauren is obsessed with sesame chicken and has made no fewer than 24,320 variations in her recipe-development career. Okay, that number may be an overstatement—but seriously, we know our sesame chicken, and we bet you're going to love this version just as much as we do!**

## SERVES 4

## NUTRITION
(per serving)

**Calories**
541 kcal

**Fat**
36.6 g

**Protein**
43.3 g

**Carbs**
10.9 g

**Fiber**
3.9 g

**Net Carbs**
7 g

### Chicken
1 large egg

2 scoops (18 g) whey protein isolate

¼ tsp sea salt

½ tsp white pepper

1½ lbs (681 g) boneless, skinless chicken thighs, cut into bite-size pieces

¼ cup (60 ml) algae or avocado oil or ¼ cup (56 g) lard or coconut oil

2 green onions, thinly sliced

2 cups (88 g) steamed broccoli florets

3 cups (360 g) cooked cauliflower rice

### Sauce
⅓ cup (80 ml) tamari

¼ cup (36 g) powdered erythritol

3 tbsp (45 ml) white wine vinegar

2 tbsp (30 ml) water

1 tbsp (15 ml) toasted sesame oil

1 (2-inch [5-cm]) piece fresh ginger, grated

2 cloves garlic, minced

¼ cup (36 g) sesame seeds

½ tsp red pepper flakes

¼ tsp sea salt

To make the chicken, whisk together the egg, whey protein isolate, salt, and white pepper in a medium bowl. Add the chicken and toss to coat.

Heat the algae oil in a 10-inch (25-cm) or larger cast iron skillet over medium-high heat. Working in batches if necessary to avoid overcrowding the skillet, add the chicken in a single layer and fry it for 3 minutes per side, until it is golden brown.

To make the sauce, whisk together the tamari, erythritol, vinegar, water, sesame oil, ginger, garlic, sesame seeds, red pepper flakes, and salt in a small bowl.

Once all the chicken is cooked, place all the chicken in the skillet. Pour the sauce over the chicken and toss to coat.

Cook the chicken for 2 to 3 minutes, or until the sauce has thickened. Add the green onions.

Serve the chicken with the broccoli and cauliflower rice.

# QUESO CHICKEN SOUP

One of the most popular and, dare we say, delicious recipes on our blog is our famous Queso Chicken Soup, so we just knew that we had to include it in this book. This soup is perfect for chilly nights, but we don't blame you for making it in the middle of July as well. If you're a topping fanatic, feel free to add even more. Avocado and sour cream are delicious in this soup!

## Soup
1 tbsp (15 ml) avocado oil
2 (10-oz [280-g]) cans Rotel Original, drained
1 tbsp (9 g) gluten-free taco seasoning
1 lb (454 g) boneless, skinless chicken breasts
3 cups (720 ml) chicken broth

8 oz (224 g) cream cheese
½ cup (120 ml) heavy cream
Sea salt, as needed

## Toppings
1 medium jalapeño pepper, thinly sliced
1 tbsp (4 g) minced cilantro

To make the soup, heat the oil in a 5-quart (4.8-L) cast iron Dutch oven over medium heat. Add the Rotel and taco seasoning and cook for 1 minute to toast the seasoning.

Add the chicken and broth, cover the Dutch oven, and simmer the mixture for 25 minutes or until the chicken's internal temperature reaches 165°F (74°C). Remove the chicken and shred it. Set it aside.

Stir the cream cheese and heavy cream into the soup. If desired, blend the soup with an immersion blender for a creamier texture. Once the cheese has melted, add the chicken back to the soup. Season with the salt and serve the soup topped with the jalapeño pepper and cilantro.

## SERVES 4

## NUTRITION
(per serving)

**Calories**
473 kcal

**Fat**
35.7 g

**Protein**
33.9 g

**Carbs**
10 g

**Fiber**
3 g

**Net Carbs**
7.1 g

**SERVES 4**

## NUTRITION

(per serving)

**Calories**
321 kcal

**Fat**
17.5 g

**Protein**
30.3 g

**Carbs**
12.1 g

**Fiber**
4.1 g

**Net Carbs**
8.1 g

# MONGOLIAN BEEF AND BROCCOLI

This classic Asian dish may remind you of takeout, but it has only a fraction of the carbs and no sacrifice in flavor. This is a great recipe for the whole family to enjoy or to prep for busy days ahead.

### Beef and Broccoli
1 lb (454 g) flank steak, cut into ¼-inch (6-mm) thick strips

1 tbsp (15 ml) tamari

1 tsp toasted sesame oil

2 tbsp (30 ml) avocado oil

2 cups (88 g) broccoli florets

4 green onions, cut into 1-inch (2.5-cm) pieces

4 cups (480 g) cooked cauliflower rice

### Sauce
1 tbsp (6 g) grated fresh ginger

4 cloves garlic, minced

¼ cup (60 ml) tamari

3 tbsp (36 g) brown erythritol

2 tsp (6 g) sesame seeds

To make the beef and broccoli, combine the steak, tamari, and sesame oil in a large glass container with a lid. Toss to coat the steak, cover the container with its lid, and refrigerate the meat for 30 minutes.

To make the sauce, whisk together the ginger, garlic, tamari, and erythritol in a small bowl. Set the sauce aside.

Heat the avocado oil in a 10-inch (25-cm) or larger cast iron skillet over medium-high heat. Add the steak and its marinade to the skillet and cook the steak for 2 minutes per side.

Pour in the sauce and bring it to a simmer. Add the broccoli and green onions.

Cook the mixture for about 5 minutes, until the green onions and broccoli have softened. Stir in the sesame seeds. Serve the beef and broccoli with the cauliflower rice.

# BLUE CHEESE AND PECAN–STUFFED PORK TENDERLOIN

Caramelized onions, blue cheese, and pecans make the perfect filling for this easy stuffed pork tenderloin. Toothpicks make quick work of securing the pork once it's rolled up, but butcher's twine will work as well if you happen to have that on hand.

**SERVES 6**

**NUTRITION**
(per serving)

**Calories**
360 kcal

**Fat**
24.6 g

**Protein**
28.8 g

**Carbs**
6.7 g

**Fiber**
2.2 g

**Net Carbs**
4.6 g

6 tbsp (90 ml) olive oil, divided

1 small white onion, chopped

1 clove garlic, minced

1 tsp minced fresh rosemary

1 tsp minced fresh thyme

1 tsp minced fresh oregano

¼ cup (34 g) crumbled blue cheese

¼ cup (27 g) crushed pecans

1½ lbs (681 g) pork tenderloin

1¼ tsp (8 g) sea salt, divided

¼ tsp black pepper

8 oz (224 g) cremini mushrooms

1 medium zucchini, cubed

1 cup (88 g) fresh Brussels sprouts

1 tbsp (14 g) unsalted butter

Preheat the oven to 400°F (204°C).

Heat 1 tablespoon (15 ml) of the oil in a 10-inch (25-cm) or larger cast iron skillet over medium heat. Add the onion and garlic and reduce the heat to medium-low. Cook, stirring frequently, for 10 to 15 minutes, until the onion is brown and very soft. Transfer the onion and garlic to a small bowl. Add the rosemary, thyme, oregano, blue cheese, and pecans to the bowl and mix until they are combined with the onion and garlic.

Place the pork tenderloin on a cutting board and make a cut down the middle, making sure to not cut all the way through. The tenderloin will open up like a book. Cover the pork with a clean tea towel and use a meat mallet to pound it out until it is ½ inch (13 mm) thick. Spread the blue cheese mixture evenly over the surface of the pork, leaving a ½-inch (13-mm) border. Roll the tenderloin up, starting at the long side, securing it with toothpicks or butcher's twine.

In the same skillet, heat 2 tablespoons (30 ml) of the oil over medium-high heat. Season the pork with 1 teaspoon of the salt and the black pepper. Sear the tenderloin for 2 minutes per side, until it has browned. Arrange the mushrooms, zucchini, and Brussels sprouts around the pork and drizzle everything with the remaining 3 tablespoons (45 ml) of oil and the remaining ¼ teaspoon of salt.

Bake the pork and vegetables for 25 minutes, or until the internal temperature of the pork reaches 150°F (66°C), then transfer the tenderloin to a cutting board and allow it to rest for 10 minutes before slicing it into rings. Then, transfer the pork and vegetables to a serving platter. Place the skillet over high heat and add the butter. Whisk the butter for 1 to 2 minutes, until it has thickened, then pour it over the pork and vegetables. Serve immediately.

# BEEF TACO SALAD SKILLET

**Taco salad meets skillet. Is it a salad or is it a skillet dinner? No one knows for sure, but one thing is certain: It is delicious no matter what you choose to call it.**

## SERVES 6

## NUTRITION
(per serving)

**Calories**
498 kcal

**Fat**
41.1 g

**Protein**
26.1 g

**Carbs**
7.4 g

**Fiber**
2.2 g

**Net Carbs**
5.3 g

### Taco Salad Skillet
3 tbsp (45 ml) avocado oil
1½ lbs (681 g) ground beef
¼ cup (40 g) diced white onion
1 medium jalapeño pepper, diced
3 tbsp (27 g) gluten-free taco seasoning
1 tsp sea salt
½ cup (120 ml) unsweetened tomato sauce

2 tbsp (30 g) tomato paste
¼ cup (48 g) sour cream
2 oz (56 g) cream cheese
1 cup (113 g) shredded sharp Cheddar cheese, divided

### Toppings
2 cups (96 g) shredded iceberg lettuce
2 medium Roma tomatoes, diced
¼ cup (23 g) pickled jalapeño peppers

To make the taco salad skillet, heat the oil in a 10-inch (25-cm) or larger cast iron skillet over medium-high heat. Add the beef, breaking it apart with a spatula or wooden spoon. Brown the beef for 6 to 7 minutes, then add the onion and jalapeño pepper. Stir to combine and cook the mixture for 2 to 3 minutes. Add the taco seasoning and salt, and cook another minute longer.

Stir in the tomato sauce, tomato paste, sour cream, cream cheese, and ½ cup (57 g) of the Cheddar cheese. Cook the mixture for 4 to 5 minutes, until the cheeses are melted.

To serve, top the beef mixture with the lettuce, remaining ½ cup (56 g) of Cheddar cheese, tomatoes, and pickled jalapeño peppers.

# STUFFED CHICKEN PARMESAN

Chicken Parmesan holds a special place in our hearts. If you read our blog, you may know what we're talking about. The story includes exploding Pyrex, apartment neighbors shrieking, and Alex taking advantage of the splattered sauce and playing dead on one of our date nights back in college. For the full rundown, you'll have to head to the website—for now, just know that we have a history with chicken Parmesan and this recipe is our redemption.

**SERVES 4**

**NUTRITION**
(per serving)

**Calories**
717 kcal

**Fat**
50.9 g

**Protein**
56.2 g

**Carbs**
7.1 g

**Fiber**
1.4 g

**Net Carbs**
5.7 g

2 (8-oz [224-g]) boneless, skinless chicken breasts

½ cup (57 g) shredded mozzarella cheese

½ cup (50 g) shredded Parmesan cheese, divided

8 fresh basil leaves

1 cup (106 g) pork rind crumbs

1½ tbsp (5 g) Italian seasoning

1 tsp sea salt

½ tsp black pepper

⅓ cup (80 ml) olive oil

1 cup (240 ml) sugar-free marinara sauce

8 oz (224 g) fresh mozzarella cheese

Preheat the oven to 425°F (218°C).

Make a lengthwise slit in each chicken breast. Combine the shredded mozzarella cheese and ¼ cup (25 g) of the Parmesan cheese in a small bowl. Stuff each chicken breast with half of the mixture and 4 basil leaves. Secure the breasts with toothpicks.

In a food processor, combine the remaining ¼ cup (25 g) of Parmesan cheese, pork rind crumbs, Italian seasoning, salt, and black pepper. Process until the ingredients are thoroughly combined. Transfer the seasoned pork rind mixture to a shallow dish.

Heat the oil in a 10-inch (25-cm) or larger cast iron skillet over medium-high heat. Dredge the chicken through the seasoned pork rind mixture and fry the chicken for 4 to 5 minutes per side, until its internal temperature reaches 165°F (74°C).

Top the chicken with the marinara and fresh mozzarella cheese. Transfer the skillet to the oven and bake the chicken for 20 minutes, until the cheese is bubbly.

# CHICKEN SALTIMBOCCA

**This Chicken Saltimbocca is packed with Italian flavors galore, plus it's a simple and impressive skillet dinner that only takes thirty minutes to whip up!**

## SERVES 4

## NUTRITION

(per serving)

**Calories**
347 kcal

**Fat**
21.6 g

**Protein**
34.2 g

**Carbs**
3 g

**Fiber**
1 g

**Net Carbs**
2 g

4 (4-oz [112-g]) chicken cutlets
⅛ tsp sea salt
8 fresh sage leaves
8 slices prosciutto
1 tbsp (15 ml) avocado oil

4 oz (112 g) asparagus tips
½ cup (75 g) cherry tomatoes
¼ cup (60 ml) fresh lemon juice
¼ cup (56 g) unsalted butter
2 tbsp (8 g) minced fresh parsley

Season the chicken with the salt and place 2 sage leaves on each piece. Wrap each piece of chicken in 2 slices of the prosciutto.

Heat the oil in a 10-inch (25-cm) or larger skillet over medium-high heat. Sear the chicken for 3 minutes per side, until the prosciutto is crispy and the chicken's internal temperature reaches 165°F (74°C). Remove the chicken from the skillet and set it aside.

Add the asparagus to the skillet and cook until it starts to soften, about 3 minutes. Add the tomatoes, lemon juice, and butter. Add the chicken back to the skillet and cook it for 3 minutes.

Top the chicken with the parsley and serve.

# SPINACH AND CHICKEN–STUFFED SPAGHETTI SQUASH

If you want to be strong to the finish, you should eat your spinach like Popeye. Luckily, these stuffed spaghetti squashes are absolutely packed with the leafy green. Classic Italian flavors plus creamy cheese make for a perfect bite.

1 (1¾-lb [795-g]) spaghetti squash

¼ cup (60 ml) olive oil

1 lb (454 g) boneless, skinless chicken breast, cubed

½ medium onion, thinly sliced

2 cloves garlic, minced

1 (15-oz [420-g]) can diced tomatoes, drained

1 lb (454 g) baby spinach

¼ cup (60 ml) heavy cream

¼ cup (25 g) grated Parmesan cheese

2 oz (56 g) cream cheese

Sea salt, as needed

Black pepper, as needed

Cut off the ends of the spaghetti squash. Place the squash on a microwave-safe plate and microwave it for 15 minutes. Carefully remove the squash from the microwave and slice it in half lengthwise.

While the spaghetti squash is cooking, heat the oil in a 10-inch (25-cm) or larger cast iron skillet over medium-high heat. Add the chicken and cook it for 5 to 7 minutes, until it starts to brown. Add the onion and garlic. Cook the mixture for 4 to 5 minutes, until the onion is soft and the chicken is brown.

Add the tomatoes and spinach. (You may need to add the spinach a little at a time as it wilts.) Cook the mixture for 5 to 7 minutes, until the spinach is completely wilted. Pour in the heavy cream, Parmesan cheese, and cream cheese. Stir to combine.

Season the mixture with the salt and black pepper. Use a fork to fluff the spaghetti squash strands, then fill each squash half with half of the chicken mixture. Serve immediately.

## SERVES 4

## NUTRITION
(per serving)

**Calories**
458 kcal

**Fat**
29.9 g

**Protein**
33.2 g

**Carbs**
16.2 g

**Fiber**
5.8 g

**Net Carbs**
10.5 g

## SERVES 4

## NUTRITION

(per serving)

**Calories**
767 kcal

**Fat**
61.8 g

**Protein**
44.3 g

**Carbs**
9.6 g

**Fiber**
2.8 g

**Net Carbs**
6.8 g

# PERFECT STEAK
## WITH BLUE CHEESE WEDGE SALAD

This recipe creates the perfect steakhouse dinner at home. We can promise that you'll want to put this blue cheese dressing on everything. Here's a trick if rib eyes are a little too expensive: Ask your butcher for chuck eye steaks! While they are similar to rib eyes in taste, they are significantly cheaper and one of our favorite cuts of beef.

**Steaks**
4 (6-oz [170-g]) rib eye steaks
Flaky sea salt, as needed
2 tbsp (28 g) unsalted butter
2 cloves garlic, crushed
1 sprig fresh rosemary, thyme, or oregano

**Chunky Blue Cheese Dressing**
4 oz (112 g) Gorgonzola cheese, crumbled
3 tbsp (36 g) sour cream

1 tbsp (15 ml) fresh lemon juice
⅓ cup (80 ml) heavy cream
Sea salt, as needed
Black pepper, as needed

**Salad**
1 large head iceberg lettuce, quartered
4 slices cooked bacon, crumbled
2 medium Roma tomatoes, diced
2 tbsp (6 g) finely chopped fresh chives

To make the steaks, pat the rib eyes dry and season them liberally with the salt.

Heat a 10-inch (25-cm) or larger cast iron skillet over high heat. Sear the steaks for 2 minutes on each side, then reduce the heat to medium-high. Add the butter, garlic, and herbs.

Flip the steaks every 30 seconds and use a spoon to baste the steaks with each flip. Cook the steaks until their internal temperature reaches your desired level of doneness: 135°F (57°C) for medium-rare; 140°F (60°C) for medium; and 145°F (63°C) for medium-well.

Allow the steaks to rest for approximately 5 minutes before slicing.

To make the chunky blue cheese dressing, combine the Gorgonzola cheese, sour cream, lemon juice, heavy cream, salt, and black pepper in a small bowl.

To make the salad, place the lettuce quarters on plates and top them with the bacon, tomatoes, chives, and chunky blue cheese dressing. Serve the salad with the sliced steak.

# SLOPPY JOE "CORNBREAD" CASSEROLE

This is one of our favorite camping recipes that's been adapted to be made in the kitchen rather than in the great outdoors over a campfire. Plus, it would be a crime to publish a cast iron cookbook without at least one "cornbread" recipe.

**SERVES 6**

**NUTRITION**

(per serving)

**Calories**
510 kcal

**Fat**
42.4 g

**Protein**
24.3 g

**Carbs**
8.4 g

**Fiber**
2.9 g

**Net Carbs**
5.5 g

### "Cornbread"
½ cup (50 g) almond flour
¼ cup (30 g) coconut flour
1 tsp sea salt
½ teaspoon baking soda
3 large eggs
½ cup (120 ml) heavy cream
¼ cup (56 g) butter, melted

### Sloppy Joe Casserole
1 tbsp (14 g) unsalted butter
1 lb (454 g) ground beef
1 tsp chili powder
1 tsp onion powder

½ tsp garlic powder
½ tsp sea salt
½ tsp red pepper flakes
¼ tsp black pepper
½ medium green bell pepper, minced
½ large yellow onion, minced
3 cloves garlic, minced
1 tbsp (15 g) tomato paste
⅔ cup (81 g) crushed tomatoes
3 tbsp (36 g) brown erythritol
1 tsp yellow mustard
½ tsp Worcestershire sauce
1 cup (113 g) shredded Cheddar cheese

Preheat the oven to 350°F (177°C).

To make the "cornbread," combine the almond flour, coconut flour, salt, baking soda, eggs, heavy cream, and butter. Stir until the ingredients are incorporated.

To make the sloppy Joe casserole, melt the butter in a 10-inch (25-cm) or larger cast iron skillet over medium-high heat. Add the beef and cook it, without stirring, for 4 minutes. Add the chili powder, onion powder, garlic powder, salt, red pepper flakes, and black pepper. Using the back of a spatula, crumble the beef and cook for 2 to 3 minutes, until it has browned.

Add the bell pepper, onion, and garlic to the skillet and cook for 3 to 4 minutes, until the vegetables have softened.

Add the tomato paste, crushed tomatoes, brown erythritol, mustard, and Worcestershire sauce and stir to combine. Simmer the casserole mixture for 3 minutes. Add the Cheddar cheese and allow it to melt. Turn off the heat.

Top the sloppy Joe mixture with the "cornbread" batter, transfer it to the oven and bake the casserole for 30 minutes, or until a toothpick inserted into the center of the "cornbread" comes out clean. Serve immediately.

# SEA

In this chapter, the freshest flavors from the ocean are on full display in dishes like Seafood Paella (page 62), Cioppino (page 65), Southern Shrimp and "Grits" (page 77), and more. Dive in with us.

# SEAFOOD PAELLA

If you're a fan of seafood, this recipe is for you. It's packed full of scallops, shrimp, mussels, and lobster, showcasing the best of the sea. This is definitely a showstopper and will be a hit at any dinner table. By replacing the traditional rice with cauliflower, you severely reduce the carbohydrates while simultaneously increasing your cruciferous veggie intake. Pro tip: If you don't have a large enough skillet, try using a Dutch oven or wok.

**SERVES 6**

**NUTRITION**

(per serving)

**Calories**
526 kcal

**Fat**
36.9 g

**Protein**
34.9 g

**Carbs**
14.4 g

**Fiber**
4.9 g

**Net Carbs**
9.5 g

6 tbsp (90 ml) olive oil, divided

11 oz (308 g) cooked chorizo sausage, cut into bite-sized pieces

8 oz (224 g) boneless, skinless chicken thighs, cut into bite-sized pieces

8 oz (224 g) jumbo shrimp, deveined, shells removed, and tails left on

1 small yellow onion, diced

1 medium green bell pepper, diced

4 cloves garlic, minced

1 tbsp (7 g) smoked paprika

1 tsp dried oregano

½ tsp sea salt

Pinch of saffron threads

1 (15-oz [420-g]) can crushed tomatoes

6 cups (720 g) uncooked cauliflower rice

2 medium lobster tails

12 mussels or clams, cleaned

1 cup (240 ml) chicken broth or water

¼ cup (36 g) frozen peas, thawed

½ cup (30 g) minced fresh parsley

1 medium lemon, thinly sliced

Heat 1 tablespoon (15 ml) of the oil in a 13¼-inch (34-cm) or larger cast iron skillet. Add the chorizo and the chicken to the oil and brown them for 4 to 5 minutes. Add the shrimp and cook them for 2 minutes per side. Remove the shrimp and set them aside.

Push the chorizo and chicken to one side of the skillet and add the remaining 5 tablespoons (75 ml) of oil to the other. Add the onion, bell pepper, and garlic. Stir together the chorizo, chicken, and vegetables. Sauté the mixture for 5 minutes, until the vegetables have softened.

Add the smoked paprika, oregano, salt, and saffron and cook the mixture for 30 seconds. Add the crushed tomatoes. Cook for 1 minute, then add the cauliflower rice.

Tuck the lobster tails and mussels into the cauliflower rice and pour the broth over the mixture. Cook for 10 minutes, until the lobster shells are bright red and the mussels have opened. Discard any mussels that did not open.

Add the shrimp back to the skillet and cook for 2 to 3 minutes, until the shrimp are reheated. Top the paella with the peas and parsley and serve it with the lemon slices on the side.

# CIOPPINO

Lauren had her first bowl of cioppino at a little hole-in-the-wall restaurant in New Orleans back in 2015. Since then she's tried to perfect an easy version at home, and this recipe is the culmination of those efforts. The bright broth with silky halibut, mussels, clams, and shrimp creates a rustic stew that's as delicious as it is pretty. Scallops are also delicious in this stew, so feel free to add them if they're a favorite of yours.

**SERVES 8**

**NUTRITION**

(per serving)

**Calories**
326 kcal

**Fat**
17.2 g

**Protein**
27 g

**Carbs**
11.5 g

**Fiber**
2.9 g

**Net Carbs**
8.7 g

½ cup (120 ml) olive oil

1 large bulb fennel, thinly sliced

1 medium onion, diced

2 medium shallots, diced

3 cloves garlic, minced

2 tsp (12 g) sea salt

1 tsp red pepper flakes

1 tsp dried oregano

½ tsp black pepper

1 cup (240 ml) dry white wine

2 tbsp (30 g) tomato paste

1 (28-oz [784-g]) can whole plum tomatoes, undrained

1 (8-oz [240-ml]) bottle clam juice

4 cups (960 ml) chicken broth

1 lb (454 g) clams, cleaned

1 lb (454 g) mussels, cleaned

1 lb (454 g) large shrimp, peeled and deveined

1 lb (454 g) halibut, cut into 2-inch (5-cm) pieces

¼ cup (15 g) finely chopped fresh parsley

Juice of 1 medium lemon

Heat the oil in a 5-quart (4.8-L) cast iron Dutch oven over medium heat. Add the fennel, onion, and shallots. Cook the vegetables, stirring frequently, for 10 minutes, until the onion is translucent.

Add the garlic, salt, red pepper flakes, oregano, and black pepper and cook the mixture for 30 seconds, until it is fragrant. Add the wine, scraping up any stuck-on bits, and allow the wine to reduce for 3 to 4 minutes. Add the tomato paste, plum tomatoes, clam juice, and broth.

Bring the mixture to a simmer, cover the Dutch oven, and cook for 20 minutes. Remove the Dutch oven's lid and add the clams and mussels. Cook the stew, uncovered, until the clams and mussels begin to open, about 5 minutes.

Add the shrimp and halibut. Cook the soup for 5 to 7 minutes, until the fish is firm, the shrimp are pink, and all of the mussels and clams have opened. Discard any closed mussels or clams.

Stir in the parsley and lemon juice and serve.

# SHRIMP CHOW MEIN

**Get your veggie fix with this chow mein! Not a fan of shrimp? Feel free to swap it for chicken—you'll just want to cook thin slices of chicken in a bit of oil or butter first, since the shrimp is precooked.**

## SERVES 4

## NUTRITION
(per serving)

**Calories**
273 kcal

**Fat**
18.5 g

**Protein**
15.4 g

**Carbs**
13.4 g

**Fiber**
4 g

**Net Carbs**
9.4 g

1 (2-lb [908-g]) spaghetti squash
2 tbsp (30 ml) tamari
1 tsp brown erythritol
1 tbsp (6 g) grated fresh ginger
2 cloves garlic, minced
2 tbsp (30 ml) toasted sesame oil
3 tbsp (45 ml) avocado oil
¼ cup (40 g) diced white onion

2 fresh Thai chiles, minced, or ½ tsp red pepper flakes
12 oz (336 g) cooked, peeled, and deveined shrimp
9 oz (252 g) coleslaw mix
1 cup (50 g) mung bean sprouts
2 green onions, thinly sliced
Sea salt, as needed

Slice off the ends of the spaghetti squash and use a fork to poke holes all over the outside. Place the squash on a microwave-safe plate and microwave for 15 minutes. Cut the squash in half lengthwise and scoop out the seeds. Use a fork to remove the "spaghetti" threads from the squash. Set the squash threads aside.

In a small bowl, whisk together the tamari, brown erythritol, ginger, and garlic. Set aside.

Heat the sesame oil and avocado oil in a 10-inch (25-cm) or larger cast iron skillet over medium-high heat. Add the onion and Thai chiles and cook until the vegetables are soft, 3 to 4 minutes. Add the shrimp and cook for 2 minutes, until they are warm. Stir in the coleslaw mix, bean sprouts, and green onions. Cook the mixture for 2 to 3 minutes, until the cabbage starts to soften.

Drain any liquid that has accumulated in the bottom of the bowl with the spaghetti squash. Add the spaghetti squash and tamari sauce to the skillet. Cook the chow mein for 3 to 4 minutes, until the sauce is absorbed. Taste the chow mein and add the salt if necessary. Serve immediately.

# SOUTHERN GUMBO

This dish is another New Orleans classic. While we're not going to pretend that this remotely comes close to replacing the real deal in flavor or texture, we can say that it is a great low-carb replacement for the beloved stew.

## SERVES 4

## NUTRITION
(per serving)

**Calories**
670 kcal

**Fat**
44.5 g

**Protein**
54 g

**Carbs**
17.8 g

**Fiber**
6.6 g

**Net Carbs**
11.2 g

¼ cup (60 ml) avocado oil

1 lb (454 g) boneless, skinless chicken thighs

8 oz (224 g) smoked andouille sausage, sliced into 1-inch (2.5-cm) pieces

¼ cup (56 g) unsalted butter

1½ tbsp (13 g) minced garlic

½ cup (80 g) diced red onion

1 medium green bell pepper, diced

2 medium ribs celery, coarsely chopped

2 tbsp (14 g) Cajun seasoning

1 (15-oz [420-g]) can fire-roasted diced tomatoes, undrained

3 cups (720 ml) low-sodium chicken broth

1 lb (454 g) shrimp, peeled and deveined

2 tbsp (30 ml) hot sauce

4 cups (480 g) cooked cauliflower rice

2 green onions, thinly sliced

2 tbsp (8 g) minced fresh parsley

Heat the oil in a 5-quart (4.8-L) cast iron Dutch oven over medium-high heat. Add the chicken and cook it for 4 for 5 minutes per side. Remove the chicken from the Dutch oven and set it aside. Add the sausage to the Dutch oven and cook it for 2 to 3 minutes per side, until it has browned. Remove the sausage from the Dutch oven and set it aside.

Reduce the heat to medium-low and add the butter, garlic, onion, bell pepper, and celery. Cook the mixture, stirring occasionally, for 10 minutes.

Add the Cajun seasoning and cook for 30 seconds, until the seasoning is fragrant. Add the diced tomatoes, broth, chicken, sausage, and their accumulated juices. Bring the gumbo to a simmer, cover the Dutch oven, and cook for 30 minutes.

Remove the chicken from the Dutch oven and transfer it to a cutting board. Shred the chicken using 2 forks, then return it to the gumbo.

Stir the gumbo and add the shrimp. Cook for 4 minutes, or until the shrimp have turned pink. Stir in the hot sauce. Taste the gumbo for seasonings and adjust as needed.

To serve, divide the gumbo among 4 bowls. Top each serving with 1 cup (120 g) of the cauliflower rice, green onions, and parsley.

**SERVES 4**

**NUTRITION**

(per serving)

**Calories**
438 kcal

**Fat**
25.5 g

**Protein**
36.2 g

**Carbs**
15.2 g

**Fiber**
5 g

**Net Carbs**
10.2 g

# SHRIMP BURGERS
## WITH HERBED SLAW

Replace your turf with surf in these shrimp burgers! We love the sweet shrimp paired with the tangy herbed slaw. This one is perfect for seafood lovers.

### Burgers

½ small red onion

½ small red bell pepper

2 large eggs

1 lb (454 g) shrimp, peeled and deveined

½ cup (53 g) pork rind crumbs

1 tsp sea salt

½ tsp garlic powder

½ tsp onion powder

½ tsp paprika

¼ cup (15 g) minced fresh herb mixture (such as cilantro, parsley, chives, and dill)

3 tbsp (45 ml) avocado oil

### Herbed Slaw

1 medium head green cabbage, shredded

2 large collard green leaves, shredded

½ small red onion, thinly sliced

½ cup (30 g) finely chopped fresh herb mixture (such as cilantro, parsley, chives, and dill)

¼ cup (34 g) capers, drained

1 cup (250 g) full-fat plain Greek yogurt

3 tbsp (45 ml) distilled white vinegar, plus more as needed

2 tbsp (30 ml) olive oil

1 tsp sea salt

½ tsp garlic powder

To make the burgers, place the onion and bell pepper in a food processor and pulse until they are minced. Add the eggs and shrimp, then pulse a few more times until the ingredients are combined. (There should be very small pieces of shrimp; the mixture should not be a paste.) Transfer the shrimp mixture to a medium bowl and stir in the pork rind crumbs, salt, garlic powder, onion powder, paprika, and herbs. Form the mixture into 4 burgers, place the burgers on a plate, and refrigerate the burgers for 30 minutes.

While the burgers are chilling, make the herbed slaw. Place the cabbage, collard greens, onion, herbs, capers, yogurt, vinegar, olive oil, salt, and garlic powder in a large bowl. Toss to combine the ingredients. Refrigerate the slaw until you are ready to serve.

Heat the avocado oil in a 10-inch (25-cm) or larger cast iron skillet over medium heat. Add the burgers to the skillet (working in batches if necessary) and cook them for 4 to 5 minutes per side, until they are golden and firm.

To serve, place the slaw on plates and top each mound of slaw with a shrimp burger.

# CREAMY CRAB BISQUE

This is such a comforting meal, we make it several times throughout the fall and winter months. You can also swap the crab for lobster, or you can go for a mixture of both if you're feeling extra adventurous. Fresh crab or lobster is best, but canned or frozen will also work in a pinch.

**SERVES 4**

**NUTRITION**

(per serving)

**Calories**
725 kcal

**Fat**
64.6 g

**Protein**
20.6 g

**Carbs**
7.6 g

**Fiber**
0.6 g

**Net Carbs**
7 g

¼ cup (56 g) unsalted butter

1 large shallot, thinly sliced

2 cloves garlic, thinly sliced

2 tbsp (30 g) tomato paste

3 tbsp (45 ml) Cognac

2 cups (480 ml) heavy cream

3 cups (720 ml) seafood stock

10 oz (28 g) cooked crabmeat, coarsely chopped, divided

¼ tsp sea salt, plus more as needed

¼ tsp cayenne pepper

Black pepper, as needed

¼ cup (12 g) finely chopped chives

¼ cup (60 ml) crème fraîche (optional)

In a 5-quart (4.8-L) cast iron Dutch oven over medium-high heat, melt the butter. Add the shallot and garlic and sauté them for 2 to 3 minutes, until they are opaque but not brown. Stir in the tomato paste and cook for 30 seconds. Pour in the Cognac to deglaze the pot. Let the mixture bubble for 30 seconds, then add the heavy cream and stock. Bring the mixture to a boil.

Add 3 ounces (84 g) of the crabmeat, salt, and cayenne pepper. Transfer the mixture to a blender and blend until it is smooth. Alternatively, use an immersion blender to blend the mixture in the Dutch oven.

Return the soup to the Dutch oven and stir in the remaining 7 ounces (196 g) of crabmeat. Cook the soup for 2 to 3 minutes, just until it is warmed through. Season the soup with additional salt and the black pepper.

To serve, top each serving with the chives and crème fraîche (if using).

**SERVES 2**

**NUTRITION**

(per serving)

**Calories**
564 kcal

**Fat**
44.1 g

**Protein**
29.7 g

**Carbs**
22.1 g

**Fiber**
9.8 g

**Net Carbs**
12.2 g

# MEXICAN SHRIMP-STUFFED POBLANOS

This spicy dinner has the perfect amount of kick from the Mexican taco seasoning, and the Poblano peppers will have the flames tickling your tongue with every bite. You can control the heat by adjusting the number of seeds you leave in the peppers.

2 tbsp (28 g) unsalted butter

½ cup (80 g) diced white onion

1 medium jalapeño pepper, diced

1 small Roma tomato, seeded and diced

1 clove garlic, minced

½ tsp sea salt

2 tsp (6 g) gluten-free taco seasoning

8 oz (224 g) shrimp, peeled, deveined, and coarsely chopped

1 tbsp (15 ml) fresh lime juice

2 oz (56 g) cream cheese, softened

½ cup (57 g) shredded Monterey Jack cheese, divided

2 large Poblano peppers, halved lengthwise and seeded

2 tbsp (8 g) finely chopped fresh cilantro

1 medium avocado, diced

Preheat the oven to 400°F (204°C).

Melt the butter in a 10-inch (25-cm) or larger cast iron skillet over medium-high heat. Add the onion, jalapeño pepper, tomato, and garlic. Cook the vegetables for 3 to 5 minutes, until they are soft. Add the salt and taco seasoning. Cook the mixture for 30 seconds, until it is fragrant. Add the shrimp and cook them for 4 minutes, until they are pink and opaque. Stir in the lime juice, cream cheese, and ¼ cup (29 g) of the Monterey Jack cheese.

Divide the mixture between the Poblano peppers and top the peppers with the remaining ¼ cup (28 g) of Monterey Jack cheese. Wipe out the skillet, then place the stuffed peppers in the skillet. Bake the peppers for 12 to 15 minutes, until the cheese is bubbly. Top the peppers with the cilantro and avocado and serve immediately.

# SOUTHERN SHRIMP AND "GRITS"

Cast iron skillets and shrimp and grits are as iconic a pair as South Carolina and humidity. What's not typically paired together are grits and Keto. However, these "grits" are made using cauliflower and will make you take back all those nasty things you used to say about cauliflower before you knew how good it could be.

## "Grits"
6 cups (720 g) uncooked cauliflower rice

3 tbsp (42 g) unsalted butter

¼ cup (60 ml) heavy cream

Sea salt, as needed

Black pepper, as needed

## Shrimp
4 slices chopped bacon

2 tbsp (28 g) unsalted butter

1 lb (454 g) shrimp, peeled and deveined

2 cloves garlic, minced

¼ tsp red pepper flakes

Sea salt, as needed

Black pepper, as needed

2 tbsp (8 g) minced fresh parsley

2 tbsp (6 g) minced fresh chives

To make the "grits," combine the cauliflower rice, butter, heavy cream, salt, and black pepper in a 10-inch (25-cm) or larger cast iron skillet over medium-high heat. Cook the "grits" for 6 to 7 minutes, until the cauliflower is soft but not mushy. Transfer the mixture to a food processor and pulse just until the consistency resembles grits. Season the "grits" with additional salt and black pepper and set them aside.

Wipe out the skillet and place it over medium heat. Add the bacon and fry it for 4 to 5 minutes, until it is crispy. Set the bacon aside.

Add the butter, shrimp, and garlic to the skillet. Cook the shrimp for 3 minutes per side, until they are opaque and cooked through. Stir in the red pepper flakes, salt, black pepper, parsley, and chives.

Divide the "grits" among 4 bowls and top each serving with the shrimp and bacon as well as any sauce left in the skillet.

## SERVES 2

## NUTRITION

(per serving)

**Calories**
586 kcal

**Fat**
51.3 g

**Protein**
24.3 g

**Carbs**
5.7 g

**Fiber**
0.1 g

**Net Carbs**
5.6 g

# SCALLOPS
## WITH BACON CREAM SAUCE

**Scallops are one of Lauren's favorite foods. Bacon is one of Alex's. This meal captures the brininess of the scallops and pairs it perfectly with a smoky, creamy sauce.**

8 oz (224 g) sea scallops

Sea salt, as needed

Black pepper, as needed

2 tbsp (28 g) unsalted butter, divided

1 tsp olive oil

3 slices bacon, chopped

½ cup (120 ml) heavy cream

¼ cup (25 g) grated Parmesan cheese

2 tbsp (6 g) finely chopped chives

Season the scallops liberally with the salt and black pepper. Heat 1 tablespoon (14 g) of the butter and the oil in a 10-inch (25-cm) or larger cast iron skillet over medium-high heat. Add the scallops and sear them for 3 minutes, until a crust has formed. Flip the scallops and cook them for another 2 to 3 minutes. Transfer the scallops to a plate and set them aside.

In the same skillet over medium heat, fry the bacon for 4 to 5 minutes, until it is crispy. Add the remaining 1 tablespoon (14 g) of butter, heavy cream, and Parmesan cheese and bring the mixture to a simmer. While whisking, cook it for 2 to 3 minutes, just until it is reduced and thick. Season the sauce with salt and black pepper. Place the scallops in the sauce, top with the chives and serve.

# PARMESAN SHRIMP SCAMPI

*Buttery* and *garlicky* are two words you could use to describe this recipe, or you could just sum it up with one word: Yum! And since you'll have leftover wine, we'll save you a Google search: 3.1 carbs per 5 ounces (150 ml).

3 tbsp (45 ml) olive oil

4 cloves garlic, thinly sliced

1 lb (454 g) large shrimp, peeled and deveined

¼ cup (60 ml) dry white wine

1 tbsp (15 ml) fresh lemon juice

¼ cup (56 g) unsalted butter

Sea salt, as needed

3 tbsp (12 g) finely chopped parsley

¼ cup (25 g) shaved Parmesan cheese

4 cups (600 g) zucchini noodles or shirataki noodles, prepared according to package directions

1 medium lemon, sliced

¼ tsp red pepper flakes (optional)

Heat the oil in a 10-inch (25-cm) or larger cast iron skillet over medium heat. Add the garlic and shrimp. Cook the shrimp for 3 to 4 minutes, until they are almost cooked through but not brown. Remove the shrimp and set them aside.

Add the wine, lemon juice, and butter to the skillet. Cook the mixture for 4 to 5 minutes, until the sauce is glossy. Return the shrimp to the skillet and season the scampi with the salt. Stir in the parsley, top the shrimp with the Parmesan cheese and place the scampi over the zucchini noodles. Top the scampi with the lemon slices and red pepper flakes (if using), and serve.

**SERVES 4**

**NUTRITION**
(per serving)

**Calories**
306 kcal

**Fat**
23.7 g

**Protein**
18.4 g

**Carbs**
4.4 g

**Fiber**
0.8 g

**Net Carbs**
3.6 g

## SERVES 4

## NUTRITION
(per serving)

**Calories**
292 kcal

**Fat**
21.2 g

**Protein**
17.5 g

**Carbs**
9.3 g

**Fiber**
2.9 g

**Net Carbs**
6.4 g

# SARDINE-STUFFED BAKED TOMATOES

**Sardines are an often-overlooked protein source rich in omega-3 fatty acids. Elevate these superfood fishes by unpacking them from the can and packing them into juicy tomatoes.**

2 (4-oz [112-g]) cans sardines, drained and minced

½ cup (60 g) uncooked cauliflower rice

¼ cup (15 g) minced fresh parsley

2 tbsp (6 g) minced fresh mint

2 cloves garlic, minced

1 tsp paprika

½ tsp ground cumin

¼ tsp sea salt

2 tbsp (28 g) minced preserved lemons

1 tbsp (15 ml) brine from preserved lemons

¼ cup (60 ml) olive oil

4 large tomatoes

Preheat the oven to 400°F (204°C).

In a large bowl, combine the sardines, cauliflower rice, parsley, mint, garlic, paprika, cumin, salt, preserved lemons, brine, and oil. Stir to incorporate the ingredients and create a filling.

Slice the tops off of the tomatoes and use a spoon to hollow out the middles. Divide the filling between the tomatoes and place them in a 10-inch (25-cm) cast iron skillet. Roast the tomatoes for 20 minutes. Serve immediately.

# CAJUN TILAPIA
## WITH RUSTIC AVOCADO SALSA

Quick and easy, this Cajun tilapia is bursting with spice and flavor. The avocado salsa cools down the heat while also providing a nice crunch.

**NUTRITION**

(per serving)

**Calories**
419 kcal

**Fat**
30.8 g

**Protein**
25.9 g

**Carbs**
14.6 g

**Fiber**
8.8 g

**Net Carbs**
5.7 g

### Tilapia
1 lb (454 g) tilapia fillets

4 tbsp (60 ml) avocado oil, divided

3 tbsp (21 g) Cajun seasoning

### Salsa
2 medium avocados, cut into eighths

1 cup (150 g) cherry tomatoes, halved

1 medium jalapeño pepper, thinly sliced

¼ medium red onion, thinly sliced

2 tbsp (30 ml) fresh lime juice

Sea salt, as needed

To make the tilapia, rub the fillets with 1 tablespoon (15 ml) of the oil and the Cajun seasoning. Heat the remaining 3 tablespoons (45 ml) of oil in a 10-inch (25-cm) or larger cast iron skillet over medium heat.

Add the tilapia to the skillet (working in batches if necessary) and cook the fish for 3 to 4 minutes per side, until it is golden and cooked through. Transfer the tilapia to a serving platter.

To create the salsa, arrange the avocados, tomatoes, jalapeño pepper, and onion over the fish in individual layers. Top the salsa with the lime juice and salt, and serve immediately.

# SHRIMP BIRYANI

**This easy Shrimp Biryani has tons of flavor and a large dose of vegetables. We've topped it off with homemade raita and cucumber for a complete meal.**

**SERVES 4**

**NUTRITION**

(per serving)

**Calories**
324 kcal

**Fat**
21.2 g

**Protein**
20.9 g

**Carbs**
15.9 g

**Fiber**
5.2 g

**Net Carbs**
10.7 g

### Shrimp
12 oz (336 g) shrimp, peeled and deveined

2 tbsp (32 g) full-fat plain Greek yogurt

1 tbsp (6 g) garam masala

1 tsp sea salt

½ tsp ground turmeric

½ tsp ground coriander

½ tsp ground cumin

### Raita
½ cup (125 g) full-fat plain Greek yogurt

2 tbsp (18 g) minced cucumber

1 tbsp (4 g) minced fresh cilantro

1 tsp fresh lemon juice

½ tsp ground cumin

### "Rice"
6 tbsp (84 g) unsalted butter, divided

½ medium red onion, thinly sliced

1 medium jalapeño pepper, thinly sliced

2 cloves garlic, minced

1 tsp grated fresh ginger

1 medium Roma tomato, coarsely chopped

6 cups (720 g) uncooked cauliflower rice

### Toppings
1 medium cucumber, thinly sliced

¼ cup (12 g) chopped fresh mint

¼ cup (15 g) chopped fresh cilantro

To make the shrimp, combine the shrimp, yogurt, garam masala, salt, turmeric, coriander, and cumin in a medium bowl. Mix well and marinate the shrimp for at least 30 minutes in the refrigerator.

Meanwhile, to make the raita, combine the yogurt, cucumber, cilantro, lemon juice, and cumin in a small bowl. Refrigerate the raita until you are ready to serve.

To make the "rice," melt 3 tablespoons (42 g) of the butter in a 10-inch (25-cm) or larger cast iron skillet over medium-high heat. Add the shrimp and the marinade and cook the shrimp for 2 minutes per side, until they are pink and opaque. Transfer the shrimp to a plate and set the plate aside.

Add the remaining 3 tablespoons (42 g) of butter, onion, jalapeño pepper, garlic, and ginger. Cook the mixture for 3 minutes, until the vegetables start to soften. Add the tomato and cauliflower rice and cook the mixture until the cauliflower rice has softened, about 7 minutes. Return the shrimp to the skillet and cook for 1 minute to reheat the shrimp.

To serve, top the biryani with the raita, cucumber, and chopped herbs.

# CHORIZO AND SCALLOP SKEWERS
## WITH TEQUILA-LIME JICAMA AND AVOCADO SLAW

Smoky chorizo pairs perfectly with briny bright scallops in these easy skewers. Don't skip the splash of the tequila in the slaw if you have it on hand. If you have mezcal, the smokiness plays great with the chorizo, so try swapping that in for regular tequila for a bit of flair.

**SERVES 4**

**NUTRITION**
(per serving)

**Calories**
558 kcal

**Fat**
46 g

**Protein**
19.1 g

**Carbs**
18.4 g

**Fiber**
9.3 g

**Net Carbs**
9 g

### Skewers
3 tbsp (45 ml) avocado oil, divided

1 medium serrano pepper

1 tbsp (1 g) fresh cilantro leaves

Sea salt, as needed

12 oz (336 g) sea scallops

3½ oz (98 g) fully cooked hard chorizo

Black pepper, as needed

### Slaw
1 small jicama, peeled and shredded

1 cup (75 g) shredded napa cabbage

½ medium red bell pepper, thinly sliced

1 medium avocado, quartered

¼ cup (60 ml) fresh lime juice

1 tbsp (15 ml) quality tequila or mezcal

1 tbsp (15 ml) rice vinegar

½ tbsp (3 g) ancho chile powder

3 tbsp (45 ml) avocado oil

⅛ cup (8 g) finely chopped fresh cilantro

Sea salt, as needed

To make the skewers, combine 2 tablespoons (30 ml) of the oil, the serrano pepper, and cilantro in a food processor and process until the serrano oil is smooth. Season the serrano oil with the salt. Set it aside.

To make the slaw, mix together the jicama, cabbage, bell pepper, avocado, lime juice, tequila, vinegar, ancho chile powder, oil, cilantro, and salt in a large bowl. Refrigerate the slaw until you are ready to serve.

Skewer the scallops and chorizo using 2 skewers for each so that the scallops lie flat. You'll end up with 4 total skewers using 8 skewers. Season the skewers with the salt and black pepper.

Grease a large cast iron grill pan with the remaining 1 tablespoon (15 ml) of oil and heat the grill pan over medium-high heat. Add the skewers to the grill pan and cook them for 4 to 5 minutes per side, until the scallops are firm and opaque and the chorizo is browned. Drizzle the skewers with the serrano oil and serve with the slaw.

# DATE NIGHT

We know that cooking for two can be hard and, if you're like Lauren, you don't necessarily live for leftovers. If this sounds like you, you're going to love these dinner-for-two recipes. We're sharing a few of our date night favorites, like Tandoori Chicken with Tomato-Mint Salad (page 95) and Chimichurri Skirt Steak with Lobster-Turnip Stacks (page 103).

## NUTRITION

(per serving)

**Calories**
809 kcal

**Fat**
65 g

**Protein**
46 g

**Carbs**
14.5 g

**Fiber**
4.5 g

**Net Carbs**
10 g

# SPINACH AND RED PEPPER–STUFFED SALMON
## WITH ROASTED GARLIC MASHED CAULIFLOWER

**The creamy spinach filling and the roasted garlic in this dish pair perfectly to create a nutritious and delicious date night that is sure to impress.**

### Mashed Cauliflower
2 tbsp (28 g) unsalted butter

3 cups (360 g) diced cauliflower

3 cloves roasted garlic

⅓ cup (80 ml) heavy cream, plus more as needed

Sea salt, as needed

Black pepper, as needed

### Salmon
2 (6-oz [168-g]) salmon fillets

1 tsp sea salt

¼ tsp black pepper

1 tbsp (15 ml) olive oil

2 oz (56 g) baby spinach

2 oz (56 g) room-temperature cream cheese

¼ cup (37 g) diced roasted red peppers

2 tbsp (10 g) grated Parmesan cheese

2 tbsp (28 g) unsalted butter

1 tbsp (15 ml) fresh lemon juice

Preheat the broiler to 500°F (260°C).

To make the mashed cauliflower, melt the butter in a 10-inch (25-cm) or larger cast iron skillet over medium-high heat. Add the cauliflower, garlic, and heavy cream. Cover the skillet and simmer the mixture for 15 minutes, until the cauliflower is soft. Transfer the mixture to a food processor or blender and process until the desired consistency is reached, adding an additional 1 tablespoon (15 ml) of heavy cream if needed. Season the mashed cauliflower with the salt and black pepper.

Transfer the cauliflower to a bowl and set aside. Wipe out the skillet.

To make the salmon, cut a slit in the side of each salmon fillet, making sure to not cut all the way through. Season the salmon with the salt and black pepper.

Heat the oil in the skillet over medium-high heat. Add the spinach and cook it just until it has wilted, 3 to 4 minutes. Transfer the spinach to a medium bowl and add the cream cheese, red peppers, and Parmesan cheese. Mix until the ingredients are combined.

Stuff each salmon fillet with half of the spinach mixture.

Melt the butter in the skillet over medium-high heat. Add the salmon, skin side down, and cook it for 5 to 6 minutes, then transfer the skillet to the oven and broil for 5 minutes, until the salmon is golden. Drizzle the lemon juice over the salmon and serve the fillets on top of the mashed cauliflower.

# TANDOORI CHICKEN
## WITH TOMATO-MINT SALAD

Tandoori chicken is one of our favorite date night meals. It has everything you could possibly want: a little bit of spice, a bed of fresh vegetables with a tangy herb dressing, and the crispy chicken with a cool yogurt raita. Searing the chicken on the stove means you'll get a crunchy skin on the chicken, while baking it in the oven for the last bit of cooking time ensures that the meat stays moist.

**SERVES 2**

**NUTRITION**

(per serving)

**Calories**
1050 kcal

**Fat**
83.7 g

**Protein**
61.9 g

**Carbs**
11.1 g

**Fiber**
2.7 g

**Net Carbs**
8.4 g

### Chicken
2 (11-oz [308-g]) bone-in, skin-on chicken legs
3 tbsp (45 ml) melted ghee, divided
1½ tbsp (9 g) garam masala
½ tsp salt

### Salad
2 medium Roma tomatoes, quartered
1 small red onion, thinly sliced
½ medium English cucumber, thinly sliced
2 medium serrano peppers, thinly sliced
1 tbsp (3 g) minced fresh mint

1 tbsp (4 g) minced fresh cilantro
3 tbsp (45 ml) avocado oil
½ tsp distilled white vinegar
Sea salt, as needed

### Raita
½ cup (125 g) full-fat plain Greek yogurt
¼ cup (33 g) diced cucumber
1 tbsp (4 g) minced fresh cilantro
¼ tsp garam masala
¼ tsp fresh lemon juice
Pinch of sea salt

To make the chicken, preheat the oven to 425°F (218°C). Drizzle the chicken legs with 1 tablespoon (15 ml) of the ghee, then coat the chicken with the garam masala and salt.

Heat the remaining 2 tablespoons (30 ml) of ghee in a 10-inch (25-cm) or larger cast iron skillet over medium-high heat. Add the chicken to the skillet and brown it for 4 minutes per side. Transfer the skillet to the oven and bake the chicken for 25 minutes.

While the chicken is baking, assemble the salad. In a medium bowl, toss together the tomatoes, onion, cucumber, and serrano peppers. Place the mint, cilantro, oil, and vinegar in a small blender and blend until smooth. Season the dressing with the salt to taste and set it aside.

To make the raita, combine the yogurt, cucumber, cilantro, garam masala, lemon juice, and salt in a small bowl and mix to combine. Refrigerate the raita until you are ready to serve.

When the chicken's internal temperature reaches 165°F (74°C), remove it from the oven. To serve, drizzle the chicken and the tomato-mint salad with the dressing and serve with the raita.

# CAPRESE SALMON SKEWERS

**These skewers are absolutely delicious, and if that's not enough for you to give them a try, think of all the flatware you won't have to wash, as this recipe barely dirties the kitchen—that means more time to enjoy your life!**

**SERVES 2**

**NUTRITION**

(per serving)

**Calories**
683 kcal

**Fat**
42.5 g

**Protein**
65.1 g

**Carbs**
7.3 g

**Fiber**
1.2 g

**Net Carbs**
6.1 g

### Salmon
12 oz (336 g) salmon, cut into 2-inch (5-cm) chunks
2 tbsp (30 ml) avocado oil
½ tsp smoked paprika
¼ tsp Italian seasoning
¼ tsp garlic salt

### Skewers
12 cherry tomatoes
8 mini balls fresh mozzarella cheese
12 fresh basil leaves
1 tbsp (15 ml) balsamic vinegar

Place the salmon in a medium bowl. Add the oil, smoked paprika, Italian seasoning, and garlic salt. Toss the ingredients together to coat the salmon with the oil and spices.

Heat a 10-inch (25-cm) or larger cast iron skillet over medium-high heat. Add the salmon and seasoned oil. Cook the salmon for 3 to 4 minutes per side, until it is crispy and the internal temperature reaches 145°F (63°C).

To assemble the skewers, gently skewer the ingredients in an alternating pattern: salmon, tomatoes, mozzarella cheese, and basil. Drizzle the skewers with the vinegar just before serving.

# CREAMY CHICKEN AND MUSHROOM PASTA

Our riff on chicken Marsala, this Creamy Chicken and Mushroom Pasta will check off your pasta craving stat. If you don't have Marsala wine on hand, you can substitute a wee bit of extra broth—but we especially like the classic Italian flavor the wine gives the dish.

2 tbsp (30 ml) olive oil

10 oz (280 g) chicken cutlets

¼ tsp sea salt

½ tsp black pepper

1½ cups (120 ml) dry Marsala wine

1 tbsp (14 g) unsalted butter

4 oz (112 g) cremini mushrooms, thinly sliced

3 cloves garlic, minced

½ cup (120 ml) heavy cream

1 (7-oz [196-g]) package shirataki linguine noodles, prepared according to package directions

1 tbsp (4 g) minced fresh parsley

Heat the oil in a 10-inch (25-cm) or larger cast iron skillet over medium-high heat. Season the chicken with the salt and black pepper. Add the chicken to the skillet and sear it for 4 minutes per side, until it is golden and its internal temperature reaches 165°F (74°C). Remove the chicken from the skillet and set the chicken aside.

Add the wine to the skillet and scrape up any stuck-on bits from the bottom. Cook for 1 to 2 minutes to allow the wine to reduce, then add the butter and mushrooms. Cook the mushrooms for 4 to 5 minutes, until they have softened. Add the garlic and cook it for 1 minute, until it is fragrant. Pour in the heavy cream and whisk to combine.

Add the chicken back to the skillet, along with any accumulated juices. Cook the chicken for 2 to 3 minutes, until it is heated through. Add the prepared noodles, then toss to combine all the ingredients. Garnish the pasta with the parsley and serve.

## SERVES 2

### NUTRITION
(per serving)

**Calories**
610 kcal

**Fat**
45.8 g

**Protein**
35.4 g

**Carbs**
9.3 g

**Fiber**
0.8 g

**Net Carbs**
8.5 g

# CARAMELIZED ONION–SMOTHERED PORK CHOPS

## WITH LEMON-GARLIC SPINACH

**In this recipe, the richness of the Gruyère and caramelized onions smothering the pork chop is complemented by the freshness and acidity of the lemon-garlic spinach for a perfectly balanced marriage of flavors.**

**SERVES 2**

**NUTRITION**

(per serving)

**Calories**
792 kcal

**Fat**
65.6 g

**Protein**
41.3 g

**Carbs**
10 g

**Fiber**
3 g

**Net Carbs**
7 g

### Pork Chops
3 tbsp (42 g) unsalted butter

1 medium yellow onion, thinly sliced

1 clove garlic, thinly sliced

1 cup (240 ml) vegetable broth, divided

1 tbsp (15 ml) olive oil

2 (5-oz [140-g]) pork chops

1 tsp poultry seasoning

¼ tsp xanthan gum

Sea salt, as needed

Black pepper, as needed

½ cup (60 g) shredded Gruyère cheese

1 sprig fresh thyme

### Lemon-Garlic Spinach
2 tbsp (30 ml) olive oil

1 clove garlic, thinly sliced

4 cups (120 g) baby spinach

2 tbsp (30 ml) fresh lemon juice

Sea salt, as needed

Black pepper, as needed

To make the pork chops, preheat the oven to 400°F (204°C). Melt the butter in a 10-inch (25-cm) or larger cast iron skillet over medium-high heat. Add the onion and garlic to the skillet and sauté them for 5 minutes.

Add 2 tablespoons (30 ml) of the broth. Reduce the heat to medium-low and cook for 10 minutes, until the onion is golden brown. Remove the onion and garlic and set them aside.

Add the oil to the skillet. Season the chops with the poultry seasoning and add the chops to the skillet. Cook them for 4 minutes per side, until they have browned. Remove the pork chops from the skillet and set them aside.

Return the onion and garlic to the skillet and add the remaining broth. Bring the mixture to a boil and whisk in the xanthan gum. Season the mixture with the salt and black pepper.

Place the pork chops back into the skillet and top them with a spoonful of the onion mixture, the Gruyère cheese, and thyme. Transfer the skillet to the oven and bake the pork chops for 10 minutes, until the cheese is melted. Transfer the chops to a platter and wipe out the skillet.

To make the lemon-garlic spinach, heat the oil in the skillet over medium-high heat. Add the garlic and cook it for 30 seconds, then add the spinach. Cook the spinach for 2 to 3 minutes, allowing it to wilt. Add the lemon juice. Season the spinach with the salt and black pepper to taste and and serve it with the pork chops.

# CHIMICHURRI SKIRT STEAK
## WITH LOBSTER-TURNIP STACKS

This is a Keto re-creation of one of the best meals we have ever shared together. The inspiration for this dish was from a restaurant we visited on our honeymoon in Tulum, Mexico. You'll have leftover chimichurri, so we recommend drizzling it over all of your meals for the next few days after making this recipe. It's delicious on fried eggs, any type of taco bowl, steamed veggies, and any grilled meat.

**SERVES 2**

**NUTRITION**
(per serving)

**Calories**
603 kcal

**Fat**
48.2 g

**Protein**
35.4 g

**Carbs**
8.4 g

**Fiber**
2.2 g

**Net Carbs**
6.2 g

### Chimichurri
1 medium shallot, minced

1 medium Fresno chile, jalapeño pepper, or serrano pepper, minced

4 cloves garlic, minced

½ cup (120 ml) red wine vinegar

1 tsp sea salt

1 tsp red pepper flakes

½ cup (30 g) minced fresh cilantro

¼ cup (15 g) minced fresh flat-leaf parsley

2 tbsp (6 g) minced fresh oregano

¾ cup (180 ml) olive oil

### Lobster-Turnip Stacks
4 tbsp (56 g) unsalted butter, divided

1 large turnip, sliced paper thin

2 cloves garlic, minced

½ tsp sea salt, plus more as needed

4 oz (112 g) cooked lobster tail or claw meat

### Steak
8 oz (224 g) skirt steak

1 tsp sea salt

Preheat the broiler to 500°F (260°C).

To make the chimichurri, combine the shallot, Fresno chile, garlic, vinegar, salt, and red pepper flakes. Let the mixture stand for 10 minutes, then whisk in the cilantro, parsley, oregano, and oil. Reserve ¼ cup (60 ml) of the chimichurri and set it aside. Store the rest in an airtight jar in the refrigerator for up to 5 days.

To make the lobster-turnip stacks, melt 2 tablespoons (28 g) of the butter in a 10-inch (25-cm) or larger cast iron skillet over high heat. Arrange the turnip slices in a spiral in the skillet, with the slices slightly overlapping one another. Melt 1 tablespoon (14 g) of the butter and add it with the garlic and salt to the top of the turnip slices. Cover the skillet and cook the turnips for 5 minutes. Uncover the skillet and transfer it to the oven. Broil the turnips for 5 minutes, until the top is crispy.

Remove the turnip slices from the skillet and set them somewhere warm. Melt the remaining 1 tablespoon (14 g) of butter. Top the turnip slices with the lobster and drizzle them with the butter and sprinkle with salt.

To make the steak, season the steak with the salt. Heat the same skillet over high heat. Grill the steak for 3 minutes per side for medium-rare. Transfer the steak to a cutting board and let it rest for 5 minutes before slicing.

Serve the steak with the lobster-turnip stacks and drizzle the steak with the chimichurri.

# EASY RAMEN FOR TWO

**This ramen is a simple recipe with complex flavors. Plus, minimal cleanup is involved, so the recipe is easy from start to finish. This dish is perfect for a cozy restaurant-quality date night at home.**

**SERVES 2**

**NUTRITION**

(per serving)

**Calories**
373 kcal

**Fat**
29.1 g

**Protein**
19.4 g

**Carbs**
12.8 g

**Fiber**
3.3 g

**Net Carbs**
9.5 g

### Ramen
2 tbsp (30 ml) avocado oil

1 tsp toasted sesame oil

2 cloves garlic, minced

2 tsp (4 g) ginger paste

½ tsp red pepper flakes

1 small baby bok choy, halved

¼ cup (28 g) shredded carrots

½ cup (86 g) shiitake mushrooms, thinly sliced

4 cups (960 ml) vegetable broth

1 tbsp (15 ml) rice wine vinegar

3 tbsp (45 ml) low-sodium tamari

1 tbsp (15 ml) sugar-free Sriracha, or to taste

1 (7-oz [196-g]) package shirataki noodles, rinsed

### Toppings
¼ cup (12 g) sliced green onions

1 medium serrano pepper, thinly sliced

1 tsp sesame seeds

2 large soft-boiled eggs, halved (optional)

Sugar-free Sriracha (optional)

To make the ramen, heat the avocado oil and sesame oil in a 5-quart (4.8-L) cast iron Dutch oven over medium heat. Add the garlic, ginger paste, and red pepper flakes and cook, stirring constantly, for 30 to 60 seconds, until the mixture is fragrant.

Add the bok choy, carrots, and mushrooms and stir to combine. Add the broth, vinegar, tamari, and Sriracha and bring the soup to a boil. Cook for 5 minutes.

Divide the noodles between 2 bowls, and ladle the soup over the noodles. Top each serving with the green onions, serrano pepper, sesame seeds, eggs, and Sriracha (if using).

# CITRUS-ROASTED CHICKEN
## WITH SHAVED FENNEL SALAD

This is one of those staple recipes that ends up on our menu at least once a week. The fennel and walnuts complement the flavors of the citrusy chicken perfectly.

**SERVES 2**

**NUTRITION**

(per serving)

**Calories**
910 kcal

**Fat**
72.8 g

**Protein**
55.5 g

**Carbs**
7.9 g

**Fiber**
2.3 g

**Net Carbs**
5.6 g

### Citrus-Roasted Chicken
2 (11-oz [308-g]) bone-in, skin-on chicken legs

2 tbsp (30 ml) olive oil

2 tsp (2 g) poultry seasoning

2 tsp (4 g) fresh lemon zest

1 tsp sea salt

¼ tsp black pepper

1 medium lemon, thinly sliced

3 cloves garlic

2 sprigs fresh oregano

### Shaved Fennel Salad
1 cup (87 g) shaved fennel

1 cup (10 g) baby arugula

¼ cup (29 g) walnuts

3 tbsp (45 ml) olive oil

1 tbsp (15 ml) red wine vinegar

1 tbsp (15 ml) fresh lemon juice

1 clove garlic, minced

¼ tsp red pepper flakes

2 oz (56 g) shaved Parmesan cheese

To make the citrus-roasted chicken, preheat the oven to 425°F (218°C).

Place the chicken legs in a 10-inch (25-cm) or larger cast iron skillet. Drizzle them with the oil.

In a small bowl, mix together the poultry seasoning, lemon zest, salt, and pepper. Divide the mixture between the chicken legs. Arrange the lemon slices, garlic, and oregano around the chicken legs.

Transfer the skillet to the oven and bake the chicken for 45 minutes, or until the internal temperature reaches 165°F (74°C).

To make the shaved fennel salad, toss the fennel with the arugula and walnuts in a medium bowl. In a small bowl, whisk together the oil, vinegar, lemon juice, garlic, and red pepper flakes. Drizzle the dressing over the salad and toss to coat. Sprinkle the salad with the Parmesan cheese.

To serve, plate the chicken with the roasted lemon and garlic along with the fennel salad. Serve immediately.

# BLACKBERRY PORK CHOPS
## WITH MASHED CAULIFLOWER

**SERVES 2**

**NUTRITION**
(per serving)

**Calories**
837 kcal

**Fat**
65 g

**Protein**
43 g

**Carbs**
22.3 g

**Fiber**
8.5 g

**Net Carbs**
13.8 g

*Berries are a great addition to savory dishes to cut through rich flavors. The blackberries in this recipe are our favorite part because of the way they pair with the garlicky cauliflower and make the pork chops shine.*

### Mashed Cauliflower
2 tbsp (28 g) unsalted butter

2 cloves garlic

4 cups (480 g) diced cauliflower

½ cup (120 ml) heavy cream

Sea salt, as needed

Black pepper, as needed

### Pork Chops
2 tbsp (30 ml) avocado oil

2 (6-oz [168-g]) boneless pork loin chops

1 tsp sea salt

¼ tsp black pepper

¼ tsp garlic powder

¼ tsp smoked paprika

¼ tsp onion powder

¼ tsp dried rosemary

¼ tsp dried thyme

¼ cup (55 g) sugar-free blackberry jam

1 tbsp (15 ml) fresh lemon juice

1 tbsp (15 ml) low-sodium tamari

⅛ tsp ground allspice

¼ cup (36 g) fresh blackberries

1 cup (100 g) steamed French green beans

To make the mashed cauliflower, melt the butter in a 10-inch (25-cm) or larger cast iron skillet over medium-high heat. Add the garlic and cook it for 30 seconds, until it is fragrant. Add the cauliflower and heavy cream. Cover the skillet and simmer the cauliflower for 15 minutes, until it is soft. Mash the cauliflower with a potato masher or blend it with an immersion blender. Season with salt and pepper to taste. Transfer it to a bowl and set aside someplace warm. Wipe out the skillet.

To make the pork chops, heat the oil in the same skillet over medium-high heat. Season the pork chops with the salt, black pepper, garlic powder, smoked paprika, onion powder, rosemary, and thyme. Sear the chops for 5 minutes per side, or until they are golden brown and their internal temperature reaches 145°F (63°C). Transfer them to a plate and set aside for 5 minutes.

To the skillet, add the jam, lemon juice, tamari, and allspice. Cook just until the sauce is hot, then add the blackberries. Cook the sauce for 1 minute, then spoon the sauce over the chops. Serve the chops with the mashed cauliflower and green beans.

# PROSCIUTTO AND ARUGULA PIZZA

**One of the earliest dates in our relationship involved us making a pizza together from scratch—a lot of laughs and a small salad-related explosion definitely made that a date to remember.**

## SERVES 2

### NUTRITION
(per serving)

**Calories**
683 kcal

**Fat**
51.5 g

**Protein**
44.1 g

**Carbs**
14.5 g

**Fiber**
3.7 g

**Net Carbs**
10.8 g

## Crust

1 cup (113 g) shredded mozzarella cheese

½ oz (14 g) cream cheese

1 large egg

½ cup (50 g) almond flour

½ tsp baking powder

½ tsp Italian seasoning

½ tbsp (7 g) butter, melted

½ tsp garlic powder

## Toppings

¼ cup (60 ml) tomato puree

4 oz (112 g) buffalo mozzarella or fresh mozzarella cheese, torn

4 slices prosciutto

4 fresh basil leaves

1 cup (10 g) baby arugula

½ tsp red pepper flakes

1 tbsp (15 ml) olive oil

Sea salt, to taste

Black pepper, to taste

Preheat the oven to 450°F (232°C).

To make the crust, combine the mozzarella cheese and cream cheese in a large microwave-safe bowl. Microwave the cheeses for 45 to 50 seconds, until they are melted. Add the egg, almond flour, baking powder, and Italian seasoning. Mix well until the dough is smooth.

Place the dough in a 10-inch (25-cm) or larger cast iron skillet and use your hands to press it into a large circle about ¼ inch (6 mm) thick. Transfer the skillet to the oven and bake the crust for 10 minutes, until its edges are starting to brown.

In a small bowl, mix together the butter and garlic powder and brush the crust with the garlic butter.

Remove the crust from the oven and top it with the tomato puree, buffalo mozzarella cheese, and prosciutto. Transfer the pizza back to the oven and bake it for 8 to 10 minutes, until the cheese is bubbly.

To serve, top the pizza with the basil, arugula, red pepper flakes, oil, salt, and black pepper.

# GOAT CHEESE–STUFFED PROSCIUTTO CHICKEN
## WITH ROASTED RADISHES

This is such a flavorful meal! We just can't get enough of these roasted radishes. And because the chicken is wrapped in prosciutto, all of the herbed goat cheese stays in place while cooking. Plus, we love the crunch of the prosciutto as well.

**SERVES 2**

**NUTRITION**

(per serving)

**Calories**
531 kcal

**Fat**
37.6 g

**Protein**
42.2 g

**Carbs**
4.2 g

**Fiber**
1.5 g

**Net Carbs**
2.7 g

2 (4-oz [112-g]) boneless, skinless chicken breasts

3 oz (84 g) herbed goat cheese

3 tbsp (45 ml) olive oil, divided

½ tbsp (2 g) poultry seasoning

4 slices prosciutto

10 medium radishes, halved

¼ tsp sea salt

⅛ tsp black pepper

1 tsp red wine vinegar

1 tsp Dijon mustard

2 cups (60 g) baby spinach

¼ cup (29 g) thinly sliced red onion

Preheat the oven to 400°F (204°C).

Make a slit in each chicken breast lengthwise, making sure to not cut all the way through. Stuff each breast with 1½ ounces (42 g) of the herbed goat cheese. Drizzle the chicken with 1 tablespoon (15 ml) of the oil and sprinkle them with the poultry seasoning. Wrap each breast with 2 slices of prosciutto and place the chicken in a 10-inch (25-cm) or larger cast iron skillet.

Arrange the radishes around the chicken and drizzle them with 1 tablespoon (15 ml) of the oil. Season the chicken and radishes with the salt and black pepper.

Transfer the skillet to the oven and bake the chicken and radishes for 35 to 40 minutes, or until the internal temperature of the chicken reaches 165°F (74°C).

In a medium bowl, whisk together the remaining 1 tablespoon (15 ml) of oil, vinegar, and mustard. Add the spinach and onion and toss to coat.

To serve, plate the chicken with the roasted radishes and the spinach salad.

# BRILLIANT BOWLS

Build-your-own-bowl restaurants are everywhere, but building your own bowl at home can be daunting, especially if you don't know where to start. Recipes like Big Mac Burger Bowls (page 120), Buffalo Shrimp Bowls (page 128), or Meat Lover's Pizza Bowls (page 123) are sure to inspire you!

# BIBIMBAP BOWLS

**Technically, this recipe could be called "bibim-cauliflower," but you won't even miss the *bap* (rice) in this Korean staple. The flavors of chile-garlic beef and the kimchi balance this dish nicely with each bite of the veggie-packed base.**

## SERVES 4

## NUTRITION

(per serving)

**Calories**
605 kcal

**Fat**
47.4 g

**Protein**
33.3 g

**Carbs**
14 g

**Fiber**
5.4 g

**Net Carbs**
8.6 g

### Chile-Garlic Beef
1 lb (454 g) rib eye steak, thinly sliced
2 tbsp (30 ml) chile-garlic sauce
1 tbsp (15 ml) avocado oil
1 tbsp (15 ml) tamari

### Mushrooms
2 tsp (10 ml) toasted sesame oil
5 oz (140 g) shiitake mushrooms, thinly sliced
Sea salt, as needed

### Spinach
1 tbsp (15 ml) avocado oil
1 clove garlic, thinly sliced
6 cups (180 g) baby spinach, loosely packed
Sea salt, as needed

### Eggs
4 tsp (20 ml) avocado oil
4 large eggs
Sea salt, as needed
Black pepper, as needed

### Bowls
3 cups (360 g) cooked cauliflower rice
1 medium carrot, shredded
1 medium cucumber, thinly sliced
2 green onions, thinly sliced
½ cup (70 g) kimchi
1 tbsp (9 g) sesame seeds

To make the chile-garlic beef, place the steak in a lidded container with the chile-garlic sauce, oil, and tamari. Refrigerate the steak for 30 minutes.

Heat a 10-inch (25-cm) or larger cast iron skillet over medium-high heat. Add the steak and the marinade and cook it for 5 to 7 minutes, until its internal temperature reaches 140°F (60°C). Remove the steak from the skillet and set it aside.

To make the mushrooms, add the sesame oil to the same skillet over medium-high heat. Add the mushrooms and cook them for 5 to 6 minutes, until they have softened. Season the mushrooms with the salt. Remove the mushrooms from the skillet and set them aside.

To make the spinach, heat the avocado oil in the same skillet over medium-high heat. Add the garlic and cook it for 30 seconds, then add the spinach. Cook the spinach for 4 to 5 minutes, until it has wilted. Season the spinach with the salt. Remove the spinach from the skillet and set it aside.

To make the eggs, heat the avocado oil in the same skillet over medium heat. Add the eggs and fry them just until the whites are set, 2 to 3 minutes. Season the eggs with the salt and black pepper.

To assemble the bowls, layer the cauliflower rice, beef, spinach, mushrooms, carrot, cucumber, green onions, and kimchi in individual serving bowls. Top each bowl with an egg and sprinkle it with the sesame seeds.

# INDIAN CHICKEN TIKKA MASALA BOWLS

This Bollywood-inspired bowl is about to become your next obsession. The chicken breast can be marinated ahead of time to make this dinner come together in a flash.

## SERVES 6

## NUTRITION

(per serving)

**Calories**
382 kcal

**Fat**
23.3 g

**Protein**
31.2 g

**Carbs**
13.4 g

**Fiber**
3.7 g

**Net Carbs**
9.7 g

### Chicken

1½ lbs (681 g) boneless, skinless chicken breasts, cut into 1-inch (2.5-cm) cubes

½ cup (125 g) full-fat plain Greek yogurt

1 tbsp (15 ml) fresh lemon juice

2½ tbsp (15 g) garam masala

1 tsp cayenne pepper

6 tbsp (84 g) unsalted butter, divided

1 small white onion, minced

1 tbsp (6 g) grated fresh ginger

3 cloves garlic, minced

1 (15-oz [420-g]) can crushed tomatoes

1 tsp sea salt

½ cup (120 ml) heavy cream

### Bowls

1 lb (454 g) cooked cauliflower rice

¼ cup (15 g) fresh minced cilantro

1 medium jalapeño pepper, thinly sliced

Place the chicken in a lidded container. Add the yogurt, lemon juice, garam masala, and cayenne pepper and stir to combine. Refrigerate the chicken for at least 30 minutes or up to overnight.

Heat 3 tablespoons (42 g) of the butter in a 10-inch (25-cm) or larger cast iron skillet over high heat. Add the chicken and its marinade to the skillet in a single layer. Cook the chicken for 3 to 4 minutes per side, until it is brown. Transfer the chicken to a plate and set it aside.

Add the remaining 3 tablespoons (42 g) of butter and allow it to melt. Add the onion, ginger, and garlic and cook them for 4 to 5 minutes, until they are soft.

Add the crushed tomatoes and salt and bring the mixture to a simmer. Add the chicken back to the skillet and simmer the mixture for 5 to 7 minutes.

Add the heavy cream to the skillet and stir to combine.

Divide the cauliflower rice and chicken tikka masala among six individual serving bowls. Top each serving with the cilantro and the sliced jalapeño pepper.

# BIG MAC BURGER BOWLS

**You're going to want to put this recipe's special sauce on everything! This bowl is a copycat of the classic Big Mac burger. While you won't find scary ingredients or tons of refined carbs in this Keto version, you will find incredible flavor.**

**SERVES 4**

**NUTRITION**
(per serving)

**Calories**
630 kcal

**Fat**
55.9 g

**Protein**
25.9 g

**Carbs**
6.9 g

**Fiber**
3.1 g

**Net Carbs**
3.8 g

### Special Sauce
½ cup (110 g) mayonnaise
¼ cup (39 g) minced dill pickles
1 tsp minced white onion
1 tbsp (15 g) ketchup
½ tbsp (8 g) yellow mustard
1 tsp distilled white vinegar
1 tsp paprika
Sea salt, as needed

### Burger
1 tbsp (14 g) unsalted butter or 1 tbsp (15 ml) avocado oil
1 lb (454 g) ground beef
1 tsp sea salt
¼ cup (50 g) minced white onion

### Bowls
8 cups (384 g) shredded lettuce
2½ oz (70 g) shredded sharp Cheddar cheese
16 dill pickle slices
1 tbsp (9 g) sesame seeds

To make the special sauce, mix together the mayonnaise, pickles, onion, ketchup, mustard, vinegar, paprika, and salt in a small bowl. Refrigerate the sauce until you are ready to serve.

To make the burger, heat the butter or oil in a 10-inch (25-cm) or larger cast iron skillet over medium-high heat. Add the beef and salt and cook for 3 to 4 minutes without disturbing it. Once the edges of the beef are crispy, use a spatula to break apart the beef. Cook it for 5 to 6 minutes, until it is cooked through. Remove the beef from the skillet and set it aside.

Turn off the heat, then immediately add the onion to the skillet. Let the onion sit in the skillet for 2 to 3 minutes to soften it.

To assemble the bowls, divide the lettuce among four individual serving bowls. Top it with the beef, Cheddar cheese, pickles, onion, and sesame seeds. Drizzle the bowls with the special sauce and serve.

# MEAT LOVER'S PIZZA BOWLS

If your favorite part of a pizza is the pineapple, then this recipe may not be for you. For the rest of us normal people, this Meat Lover's Pizza Bowl is as beefy and meaty as anything labeled "meat lover's" should be.

4 slices bacon, coarsely chopped

8 oz (224 g) ground beef

½ tsp sea salt

1 medium green bell pepper, thinly sliced

½ small red onion, thinly sliced

3 tbsp (45 ml) olive oil

2 cloves garlic, minced

1 tbsp (3 g) Italian seasoning

½ tsp red pepper flakes

1 cup (121 g) crushed tomatoes

¼ cup (25 g) sliced black olives

4 oz (112 g) sliced pepperoni

4 oz (112 g) sugar-free sliced deli ham

¼ cup (25 g) sliced pepperoncini peppers

4 oz (112 g) shredded mozzarella cheese

Heat a 10-inch (25-cm) or larger cast iron skillet over medium-high heat. Add the bacon and cook it for 3 to 5 minutes, until it is crispy. Remove the bacon from the skillet and set it aside. Reduce the heat to medium.

Add the beef and salt to the skillet. Use the back of a spatula or spoon to crumble the beef and cook it for 7 to 10 minutes, until it has browned. Remove the beef and set it aside with the bacon. Drain all but 3 tablespoons (45 ml) of fat from the skillet and add the bell pepper and onion. Sauté them for 4 to 5 minutes, just until they start to soften. Remove the vegetables and set them aside.

Add the oil, garlic, Italian seasoning, and red pepper flakes to the skillet. Cook, stirring constantly, for 30 seconds. Add the crushed tomatoes. Stir the mixture well and cook just until it is hot, about 3 minutes.

Divide the bacon and beef among four individual serving bowls. Top the bacon and beef with the black olives, pepperoni, ham, pepperoncini peppers, bell pepper and onion mixture, tomato sauce, and mozzarella cheese. Serve the bowls immediately or store them, covered, in the refrigerator for up to 4 days.

## SERVES 4

### NUTRITION
(per serving)

**Calories**
576 kcal

**Fat**
46.2 g

**Protein**
32.3 g

**Carbs**
7.7 g

**Fiber**
1.9 g

**Net Carbs**
5.8 g

# BUDDHA BOWLS

**Quiet any critic who says that the Keto diet isn't healthy with this high-fat, low-carb Buddha Bowl. Packed full of fiber, micronutrients, and healthy fats, this vegetable-heavy bowl has a macronutrient breakdown of more than 80 percent fat and less than 10 percent carbohydrates.**

## Bowls

1 cup (88 g) halved fresh Brussels sprouts

1 cup (44 g) broccoli florets

1 cup (107 g) cauliflower florets

1 medium red onion, quartered

1 medium carrot, cut into ½-inch (13-mm) rounds

1 cup (70 g) halved cremini mushrooms

3 tbsp (45 ml) olive oil

1 tsp sea salt

4 large hard-boiled eggs, halved

2 medium avocados, diced

## Spicy Green Sauce

¼ cup (60 ml) avocado oil

⅛ cup (30 g) tahini

1 cup (16 g) fresh cilantro leaves

1 clove garlic

1 medium serrano pepper

Juice of 1 medium lime

Sea salt, as needed

To make the bowls, preheat the oven to 400°F (204°C). Place the Brussels sprouts, broccoli, cauliflower, onion, carrot, and mushrooms in a 10-inch (25-cm) or larger cast iron skillet and drizzle them with the olive oil and season them with the salt. Roast the vegetables for 35 minutes, until the vegetables are brown and the carrots are tender.

To make the spicy green sauce, combine the avocado oil, tahini, cilantro, garlic, serrano pepper, lime juice, and salt in a blender or food processor and pulse until the ingredients are smooth.

To serve, divide the vegetables among four individual serving bowls. Top each bowl of vegetables with the eggs, avocados, and the spicy green sauce. Serve immediately.

# CHIMICHURRI SALMON BOWLS

Rarely a week goes by without us making this Chimichurri Salmon Bowl. After you try them, chimichurri and pickled onions will become a staple in your fridge, and you'll be able to throw this dinner together even on the busiest night of the week.

**SERVES 4**

## NUTRITION
(per serving)

**Calories**
706 kcal

**Fat**
57.3 g

**Protein**
30.3 g

**Carbs**
18.4 g

**Fiber**
5.2 g

**Net Carbs**
13.3 g

## Turmeric Pickled Onions
1 small white onion, halved and thinly sliced

¾ cup (180 ml) boiling water

½ cup (120 ml) apple cider vinegar

¾ tsp kosher salt

1 tsp ground turmeric

3 whole cloves

## Chimichurri
1 medium shallot, minced

1 medium Fresno chile, jalapeño pepper, or serrano pepper, minced

4 cloves garlic, minced

½ cup (120 ml) red wine vinegar

1 tsp sea salt

1 tsp red pepper flakes

½ cup (30 g) minced fresh cilantro

¼ cup (15 g) minced fresh flat-leaf parsley

2 tbsp (6 g) minced fresh oregano

¾ cup (180 ml) olive oil

## Salmon and Vegetables
2 tbsp (30 ml) avocado oil

1 lb (454 g) salmon fillet

1 tsp sea salt

1 large summer squash, cut into half-moons

1 cup (150 g) cherry tomatoes

## Bowls
4 cups (200 g) torn kale

1 medium Persian cucumber, diced

2 tbsp (16 g) roasted pepitas

To make the turmeric pickled onions, place the sliced onion in a large jar. Pour the boiling water over the onions and add the apple cider vinegar, salt, turmeric, and cloves. Use a spoon to push down on the onions to make sure they are submerged. Let the onions stand for 30 minutes.

To make the chimichurri, combine the shallot, Fresno chile, garlic, red wine vinegar, salt, red pepper flakes, cilantro, parsley, oregano, and olive oil in a medium bowl and mix well. Measure out ½ cup (120 ml) of the chimichurri and set it aside. Transfer the remaining chimichurri to a jar and reserve it for another use.

To make the salmon and vegetables, heat the avocado oil in a 10-inch (25-cm) or larger cast iron skillet over medium-high heat. Season the salmon fillet with the salt. Place the salmon, skin side down, into the skillet. Arrange the squash and tomatoes around the salmon. Cook the mixture for 4 to 5 minutes, until the salmon easily releases from the skillet. Flip the salmon and cook it for 4 to 5 minutes, until it is medium-rare. Transfer the salmon to a cutting board and cut it into large pieces. Cook the squash and tomatoes for 5 minutes after removing the salmon.

To assemble the bowls, fill each bowl with the salmon, squash, and tomatoes. Top the salmon and roasted vegetables with the kale, cucumber, and pepitas. Top each bowl with 2 tablespoons (30 ml) of the chimichurri and turmeric pickled onions.

# BUFFALO SHRIMP BOWLS

Alex loves Buffalo sauce. In fact, we have an entire shelf in our refrigerator devoted to Buffalo sauce. Okay, that may be a bit of an exaggeration—but a bottle never lasts long in our house, and these Buffalo Shrimp Bowls are a big reason why.

### Ranch Dressing
¼ cup (55 g) mayonnaise

1 tbsp (15 ml) fresh lemon juice

1 tsp dried parsley

1 tsp dried chives

1 tsp dried dill

¼ tsp garlic salt

¼ tsp onion powder

¼ tsp black pepper

### Buffalo Shrimp
1 large egg

¼ cup (25 g) whey protein isolate

¼ tsp sea salt

½ tsp white pepper

¼ cup (60 ml) avocado oil

1 lb (454 g) shrimp, peeled and deveined

3 tbsp (42 g) unsalted butter

¼ cup (60 ml) plus 2 tbsp (30 ml) Frank's RedHot

### Bowls
6 cups (330 g) butter lettuce leaves

½ cup (38 g) shredded red cabbage

2 medium ribs celery, diced

2 green onions, thinly sliced

¼ small red onion, thinly sliced

1 large carrot, shaved

1 medium avocado, diced

4 oz (112 g) blue cheese, crumbled

To make the ranch dressing, combine the mayonnaise, lemon juice, parsley, chives, dill, garlic salt, onion powder, and black pepper in a small jar. Secure the lid on the jar and shake it to combine the ingredients. If needed, add 1 to 2 teaspoons (5 to 10 ml) of water to thin the dressing. Refrigerate the dressing until you are ready to serve.

To make the Buffalo shrimp, whisk together the egg, whey protein isolate, salt, and white pepper in a medium bowl. Heat the oil in a 10-inch (25-cm) or larger cast iron skillet over medium-high heat. Add the shrimp to the bowl with the egg mixture and toss to combine. Transfer the shrimp to the skillet in a single layer, frying them for 1 to 2 minutes per side, until they are crispy and opaque.

Add the butter and Frank's RedHot to the skillet. Stir to combine and cook the mixture for 1 to 2 minutes, until the sauce is hot.

To assemble the bowls, divide the lettuce, cabbage, celery, green onions, red onion, carrot, avocado, and blue cheese among four individual serving bowls. Top each bowl with the shrimp. Drizzle each bowl with the ranch dressing and serve.

# GREEK CHICKEN BOWLS

This dish is one of Alex's personal favorites—but if you put enough olives and feta on top, he'd eat just about anything. Combining all the benefits of the Mediterranean diet and Keto diet in one bowl, these Greek Chicken Bowls will soon become a favorite of yours too.

**SERVES 4**

**NUTRITION**
(per serving)

**Calories**
492 kcal

**Fat**
34.6 g

**Protein**
35.8 g

**Carbs**
8.6 g

**Fiber**
1.7 g

**Net Carbs**
6.9 g

### Chicken
1 lb (454 g) boneless, skinless chicken breast, cut into 1-inch (2.5-cm) cubes
3 tbsp (45 ml) olive oil
2 tbsp (30 ml) lemon juice
1 tbsp (15 ml) red wine vinegar
1 tbsp (3 g) Greek seasoning
¼ tsp sea salt

### Tzatziki
8 oz (224 g) full-fat plain Greek yogurt
½ medium Persian cucumber, grated
2 cloves garlic, grated
Zest of 1 medium lemon
1 tbsp (15 ml) fresh lemon juice

2 tbsp (8 g) minced fresh dill
Sea salt, as needed
Black pepper, as needed

### Red Wine Vinegar Dressing
3 tbsp (45 ml) olive oil
1 tbsp (15 ml) red wine vinegar
1 tsp minced fresh oregano
Sea salt, to taste

### Toppings
1 large Persian cucumber, diced
1 cup (150 g) cherry tomatoes, halved
½ cup (58 g) thinly sliced red onion
⅓ cup (33 g) pitted Kalamata olives
4 oz (112 g) feta cheese, crumbled

To make the chicken, combine the chicken, oil, lemon juice, vinegar, Greek seasoning, and salt in a sealable container. Marinate the chicken in the refrigerator for 30 minutes or up to overnight.

To make the tzatziki, stir together the yogurt, cucumber, garlic, lemon zest, lemon juice, dill, salt, and black pepper in a medium bowl. Refrigerate the tzatziki until you are ready to serve.

Heat a 10-inch (25-cm) or larger cast iron skillet over medium-high heat. Add the chicken and marinade to the skillet. Cook the chicken for 3 to 4 minutes per side, until it is brown and its internal temperature reaches 165°F (74°C).

To make the red wine vinegar dressing, whisk together the oil, vinegar, oregano, and salt in a small bowl.

To assemble the bowls, divide the chicken among four individual serving bowls. Top the chicken with the cucumber, tomatoes, onion, olives, and feta cheese. Pour the red wine vinegar dressing over the bowls and top each bowl with the tzatziki just before serving.

## SERVES 2

## NUTRITION
(per serving)

**Calories**
824 kcal

**Fat**
37.6 g

**Protein**
48.7 g

**Carbs**
23.5 g

**Fiber**
12.2 g

**Net Carbs**
11.3 g

# SWEET CHILI SALMON BOWLS
## WITH EDAMAME AND COCONUT CAULIFLOWER RICE

Salmon is one of our go-to proteins for its healthy fats, buttery flavor, and quick cooking time. The sweet chili sauce in this bowl is the icing on the cake—um, fish—and goes perfectly with the crunchy slaw and edamame.

### Slaw
1 cup (75 g) shredded green cabbage
½ medium red bell pepper, thinly sliced
1 green onion, thinly sliced
2 tbsp (28 g) mayonnaise

### Sweet Chili Sauce
3 tbsp (45 ml) distilled white vinegar
2 tbsp (30 ml) water
2 tbsp (20 g) granulated erythritol
1 clove garlic, minced
½ tsp minced fresh ginger
⅛ tsp cayenne pepper
Pinch of sea salt

### Salmon
2 tbsp (28 g) coconut oil
2 (6-oz [168-g]) salmon fillets
½ tsp sea salt

### Coconut Cauliflower Rice
1 tbsp (14 g) coconut oil
12 oz (336 g) uncooked cauliflower rice
2 tbsp (30 ml) unsweetened coconut cream
2 tbsp (28 g) unsweetened shredded coconut, toasted

1 cup (118 g) cooked and shelled edamame

To make the slaw, combine the cabbage, bell pepper, green onion, and mayonnaise in a medium bowl. Refrigerate until ready to serve.

To make the sweet chili sauce, combine the vinegar, water, erythritol, garlic, ginger, cayenne pepper, and salt in a 10-inch (25-cm) or larger cast iron skillet over low heat. Bring the mixture to a simmer and cook for 4 to 5 minutes, stirring occasionally, until the sauce has thickened. Add 1 teaspoon of the sauce to the slaw and toss the slaw to combine it with the sauce, and transfer it back to the refrigerator. Transfer the remaining sauce to a small jar or bowl and set it aside.

To make the salmon, add the coconut oil to the skillet and allow it to melt. Season the salmon with the salt and add the salmon to the skillet, skin side down. Sear the salmon for 5 minutes, flip it, and cook it for 3 to 4 minutes more for medium-rare. Drizzle the salmon with the remaining sauce, then remove it from the skillet and set it aside.

To make the coconut cauliflower rice, melt the coconut oil in the skillet. Add the cauliflower rice and cook, stirring occasionally, for 5 minutes, until it starts to become crispy. Add the coconut cream and cook for 1 minute.

To assemble the bowls, divide the coconut cauliflower rice between two individual serving bowls. Top the cauliflower rice with the toasted coconut, a piece of salmon, half of the edamame, and half of the slaw.

# SENSATIONAL SALADS

You can say goodbye to boring salads forever, because we are leaving bland land behind and are heading to salad city. In this chapter, you'll find mouthwatering salads such as Ahi Tuna Poke Salad (page 140), Cajun Citrus Salmon Salad with Avocado (page 148), and Surf and Turf Caesar Salad (page 143).

## SERVES 4

## NUTRITION
(per serving)

**Calories**
379 kcal

**Fat**
29.3 g

**Protein**
23.5 g

**Carbs**
7.8 g

**Fiber**
2.2 g

**Net Carbs**
5.6 g

# VIETNAMESE CHICKEN NOODLE SALAD

**Just wait until you try this salad's dressing—it will blow you away with its shallot-y deliciousness. Using a rotisserie chicken in this recipe cuts down on the prep time and leaves you with minimal cleanup after dinner.**

### Salad
¼ cup (60 ml) plus 2 tbsp (30 ml) avocado oil

1 large shallot, thinly sliced

3 cloves garlic, thinly sliced

Pinch of sea salt

2 cups (150 g) shredded green cabbage

¼ cup (13 g) bean sprouts

¼ cup (28 g) shredded carrots

1 medium jalapeño pepper, thinly sliced (14 g)

3 tbsp (12 g) minced fresh cilantro

2 tbsp (6 g) minced fresh mint

2 tbsp (10 g) minced fresh Thai basil

12 oz (336 g) shredded rotisserie chicken

2 (7-oz [196-g]) packages shirataki noodles, prepared according to package directions

### Nuoc Cham Dressing
2 tbsp (30 ml) fish sauce

1 tbsp (15 ml) fresh lime juice

1 tbsp (6 g) grated fresh ginger

2 tsp (7 g) granulated erythritol

2 green onions, minced

To make the salad, heat the oil in a 10-inch (25-cm) or larger cast iron skillet over medium-low heat. Add the shallot, garlic, and salt and cook the mixture for 2 to 3 minutes, until the shallot and garlic are golden brown. Using a slotted spoon, transfer the shallot and garlic to a plate lined with paper towels and reserve the oil in the skillet.

To make the nuoc cham dressing, whisk together the reserved oil, fish sauce, lime juice, ginger, erythritol, and green onions in a small bowl. Set the bowl aside.

In a large bowl, toss together the cabbage, bean sprouts, carrots, jalapeño pepper, cilantro, mint, Thai basil, chicken, and fried shallot and garlic. Add the prepared shirataki noodles. Drizzle the dressing over the salad and toss. Divide the salad among four plates and serve.

# HARVEST STEAK SALAD

Savory steak, charred Brussels sprouts, and Gorgonzola cheese are perfectly balanced by fresh vegetables and tangy vinaigrette in this Harvest Steak Salad. Finally, pecans and pepitas add a nice crunch to this nourishing meal.

**SERVES 2**

**NUTRITION**

(per serving)

**Calories**
897 kcal

**Fat**
78.7 g

**Protein**
38.8 g

**Carbs**
13.3 g

**Fiber**
4.5 g

**Net Carbs**
8.8 g

## Salad

3 tbsp (45 ml) olive oil, divided

1 cup (88 g) halved fresh Brussels sprouts

1 tsp sea salt, plus more as needed, divided

1 tsp black pepper, plus more as needed, divided

1 (20-oz [560-g]) rib eye steak

6 cups (60 g) arugula

6 cups (300 g) coarsely chopped kale

4 oz (112 g) crumbled Gorgonzola cheese

½ cup (55 g) pecan halves

¼ cup (32 g) roasted or raw pepitas

¼ cup (12 g) unsweetened dried cranberries

¼ cup (29 g) thinly sliced red onion

## Mustard Vinaigrette

⅓ cup (80 ml) olive oil

1 tbsp (15 ml) white wine vinegar

1 tbsp (16 g) Dijon mustard

Sea salt, as needed

Black pepper, as needed

To make the salad, heat the oil in a 10-inch (25-cm) or larger cast iron skillet over high heat. Add the Brussels sprouts cut side down. Season them with salt and black pepper as needed. Cook the Brussels sprouts for 3 to 5 minutes, until they are starting to char. Stir the Brussels sprouts and move them to one side of the skillet.

Season the steak with the remaining 1 teaspoon of salt and remaining 1 teaspoon of black pepper. Add the steak to the skillet and sear it for 2 minutes on each side. Reduce the heat to medium-high. Flip the steak every 30 seconds and use a spoon to baste the steak with each flip. Cook until the steak's internal temperature reaches your desired level of doneness: 135°F (57°C) for medium-rare; 140°F (60°C) for medium; and 145°F (63°C) for medium-well.

Remove the steak from the skillet and allow it to rest for approximately 5 minutes before slicing it.

Meanwhile, make the mustard vinaigrette. In a small bowl, whisk together the oil, vinegar, mustard, salt, and black pepper.

Divide the arugula and kale between two individual serving bowls and top the greens with the Brussels sprouts, Gorgonzola cheese, pecans, pepitas, cranberries, and onion. Top each salad with the sliced steak and mustard vinaigrette and serve.

# AHI TUNA POKE SALAD

Whip together this Ahi Tuna Poke Salad, which will rival anything you get from that poke place down the street, and after one taste you'll start putting the spicy wasabi mayonnaise on everything. Reminder: You'll want to grab sushi-grade tuna for this recipe.

**SERVES 2**

**NUTRITION**

(per serving)

**Calories**
795 kcal

**Fat**
64.1 g

**Protein**
38.2 g

**Carbs**
20.5 g

**Fiber**
12.5 g

**Net Carbs**
8 g

### Spicy Wasabi Mayonnaise
1 tsp wasabi powder
2 to 3 tsp (10 to 15 ml) sugar-free Sriracha
¼ cup (55 g) mayonnaise

### Salad
1 (8-oz [224-g]) sushi-grade ahi tuna fillet
¼ tsp sea salt
1 tbsp (9 g) sesame seeds
3 tbsp (42 g) coconut oil

4 cups (120 g) salad greens
1 medium avocado, diced
½ cup (59 g) shelled and cooked edamame
1 small cucumber, thinly sliced
4 medium radishes, thinly sliced
2 green onions, thinly sliced
1 medium jalapeño pepper, thinly sliced
1 tbsp (7 g) furikake

To make the spicy wasabi mayonnaise, whisk together the wasabi powder, Sriracha, and mayonnaise in a small bowl. Set the bowl aside.

To make the salad, season the ahi tuna with the salt. Press the sesame seeds onto the fish, creating a crust. Heat the coconut oil in a 10-inch (25-cm) or larger cast iron skillet over medium heat. Sear the fish for 2 minutes per side. The inside should still be rare.

Transfer the fish to a cutting board and slice it into thin pieces.

Divide the salad greens between two individual serving bowls. Top the greens with the avocado, edamame, cucumber, radishes, green onions, jalapeño pepper, and furikake. Top the salads with the fish and a drizzle of the spicy wasabi mayonnaise.

# SURF AND TURF CAESAR SALAD

Tender steak and buttery scallops make this Surf and Turf Caesar the ultimate take on a Keto salad. Packed with leafy greens, quality protein, and healthy fats from the homemade Caesar dressing, this recipe is sure to become a new favorite.

**SERVES 2**

**NUTRITION**
(per serving)

**Calories**
913 kcal

**Fat**
78.5 g

**Protein**
43.7 g

**Carbs**
12.3 g

**Fiber**
4.5 g

**Net Carbs**
7.8 g

### Caesar Dressing
3 oil-packed anchovy fillets, finely chopped

1 clove garlic, minced

¼ tsp kosher salt

1 large egg yolk

2 tbsp (30 ml) fresh lemon juice

¾ tsp Dijon mustard

¼ cup (60 ml) plus 2 tbsp (30 ml) avocado oil

3 tbsp (15 g) grated Parmesan cheese

### Salad
2 tbsp (30 ml) avocado oil

1 (8-oz [224-g]) skirt steak

4 large sea scallops

Sea salt, as needed

Black pepper, as needed

6 cups (288 g) coarsely chopped romaine lettuce

¼ cup (23 g) thinly sliced roasted red peppers

2 tbsp (10 g) shaved Parmesan cheese

Lemon wedges, as needed

To make the Caesar dressing, whisk together the anchovy fillets, garlic, salt, egg yolk, lemon juice, and mustard in a small bowl. While whisking, drizzle in the oil a bit at a time, until the dressing is emulsified. Stir in the Parmesan cheese. Refrigerate the dressing until you are ready to use it.

To make the salad, heat the oil in a 10-inch (25-cm) or larger cast iron skillet over medium-high heat. Season the steak and scallops liberally with the salt and black pepper. Add the steak to the skillet and cook it for 3 to 4 minutes per side, or until the steak reaches your desired doneness: 125°F (52°C) for rare; 135°F (57°C) for medium-rare; 145°F (63°C) for medium; 150°F (66°C) for medium-well; and 160°F (71°C) for well done. Transfer the steak to a cutting board and let it rest for 5 to 10 minutes before slicing it.

Add the scallops to the skillet and cook them for 2 minutes per side, or until a golden crust has formed on the sides and the centers are opaque.

In a large salad bowl, toss together the lettuce and roasted red peppers with the dressing. Top the salad with the Parmesan cheese. Add the steak and scallops and serve with the lemon wedges.

# HERBED SHRIMP COBB SALAD

**The bacon, blue cheese, and butter lettuce make this a quintessential Cobb salad, but the herbed shrimp make it absolutely delicious. Never suffer through a boring salad again with this recipe in your arsenal.**

## SERVES 2

## NUTRITION
(per serving)

**Calories**
635 kcal

**Fat**
46.8 g

**Protein**
40.8 g

**Carbs**
17.1 g

**Fiber**
9.1 g

**Net Carbs**
8 g

### Blue Cheese Dressing
1 oz (28 g) blue cheese, crumbled
2 tbsp (24 g) sour cream
1 tbsp (15 ml) fresh lemon juice
2 tbsp (30 ml) heavy cream
Sea salt, as needed
Black pepper, as needed

### Salad
4 slices bacon, coarsely chopped
8 oz (224 g) shrimp, peeled and deveined
2 tsp (2 g) Italian seasoning
¼ tsp sea salt
4 cups (220 g) coarsely chopped butter lettuce
2 large hard-boiled eggs, quartered
1 medium avocado, thinly sliced
½ cup (75 g) cherry tomatoes, halved
¼ cup (29 g) thinly sliced red onion
¼ cup (34 g) crumbled blue cheese

To make the blue cheese dressing, whisk together the blue cheese, sour cream, lemon juice, heavy cream, salt, and black pepper in a small bowl or jar. Refrigerate the dressing until you are ready to serve.

To make the salad, heat a 10-inch (25-cm) or larger cast iron skillet over medium heat. Fry the bacon for 4 to 5 minutes, until it is crispy. Remove the bacon from the skillet and set it aside. Leave the bacon grease in the skillet.

Season the shrimp with the Italian seasoning and salt. Add the shrimp to the skillet and cook them for 2 minutes per side, until they are pink and opaque.

In two individual serving bowls, top the lettuce with the eggs, avocado, tomatoes, onion, blue cheese, bacon, and shrimp. Drizzle the salad with the dressing and serve.

# CRANBERRY-AVOCADO SALAD

Simplicity at its finest, this Cranberry-Avocado Salad with creamy poppy seed dressing can be whipped together in less than twenty minutes for a deliciously fresh meal.

**SERVES 2**

**NUTRITION**

(per serving)

**Calories**
737 kcal

**Fat**
60.4 g

**Protein**
33.3 g

**Carbs**
21.3 g

**Fiber**
11.2 g

**Net Carbs**
10.1 g

## Creamy Poppy Seed Dressing

¼ cup (36 g) powdered erythritol

1½ tbsp (23 ml) distilled white vinegar

¼ tsp sea salt

¼ tsp ground mustard

½ tsp grated onion

½ tsp poppy seeds

3 tbsp (45 ml) algae oil

## Salad

1 (8-oz [224-g]) boneless, skinless chicken breast

1 tbsp (3 g) Italian seasoning

1 tsp sea salt

2 tbsp (30 ml) olive oil

3 cups (165 g) coarsely chopped butter lettuce

3 cups (90 g) baby spinach

1 medium avocado, cut into eighths

¼ cup (12 g) unsweetened dried cranberries

¼ cup (27 g) sliced or slivered almonds

To make the creamy poppy seed dressing, whisk together the erythritol, vinegar, salt, mustard, onion, poppy seeds, and algae oil in a medium jar or bowl. Refrigerate the dressing until you are ready to serve.

To make the salad, season the chicken with the Italian seasoning and salt. Heat the olive oil in a 10-inch (25-cm) or larger cast iron skillet over medium heat. Sear the chicken for 5 to 6 minutes per side, until it is golden and its internal temperature reaches 165°F (74°C). Transfer the chicken to a cutting board and thinly slice it.

In two individual serving bowls, top the butter lettuce and spinach with the avocado, cranberries, almonds, and chicken. Drizzle the salad with the dressing and serve.

## SERVES 2

## NUTRITION
(per serving)

**Calories**
790 kcal

**Fat**
61.9 g

**Protein**
42.2 g

**Carbs**
21.5 g

**Fiber**
10.6 g

**Net Carbs**
10.9 g

# CAJUN CITRUS SALMON SALAD
## WITH AVOCADO

*Jazz things up with this Big Easy–inspired Cajun Citrus Salmon Salad. It's perfect for a busy weeknight and packs a flavor punch that'll leave you wanting more.*

2 tbsp (30 ml) avocado oil

1 (8-oz [224-g]) salmon fillet

1½ tbsp (11 g) Cajun seasoning

1 large head frisée or butter lettuce

1 small orange, segmented

1 medium avocado, thinly sliced

1 medium jalapeño or serrano pepper, thinly sliced

2 tbsp (8 g) minced fresh cilantro

2 oz (56 g) crumbled queso fresco

2 tbsp (16 g) roasted or raw pepitas

2 tbsp (30 ml) olive oil

Juice of 1 medium lime

Sea salt, as needed

Black pepper, as needed

Heat the avocado oil in a 10-inch (25-cm) or larger cast iron skillet over medium-high heat. Season the salmon with the Cajun seasoning. Place the salmon in the skillet skin side down. Sear the salmon for 5 minutes, flip it, and cook for 5 minutes more. Remove the salmon from the skillet and set it aside.

Place the frisée on a serving platter and top it with the orange, avocado, jalapeño pepper, cilantro, queso fresco, and pepitas.

Drizzle the salad with the olive oil and lime juice, and season it with the salt and black pepper.

Top the salad with the salmon and serve.

# THAI LARB SALAD

This Thai Larb Salad is basically just an Asian meat salad, and it's packed with intense flavors from the herbs and fish sauce. Next time, instead of ordering takeout, make dinner at home and make it this delicious Keto salad.

**SERVES 4**

**NUTRITION**
(per serving)

**Calories**
405 kcal

**Fat**
31.7 g

**Protein**
21.4 g

**Carbs**
9.1 g

**Fiber**
2.9 g

**Net Carbs**
6.1 g

1 lb (454 g) ground pork

1 small onion, minced

1 medium shallot, minced

1 clove garlic, minced

Juice of 1 medium lime

1 tbsp (15 ml) fish sauce

1 tbsp (15 g) red pepper flakes

1 tbsp (10 g) granulated erythritol

2 tbsp (28 g) coconut oil or lard

2 green onions, cut into 1-inch (2.5-cm) pieces

Pinch of salt (optional)

2 tbsp (6 g) minced fresh mint

2 tbsp (8 g) minced fresh cilantro

16 butter lettuce leaves

1 medium Persian cucumber, thinly sliced

Place the pork, onion, shallot, and garlic in a food processor and pulse until the pork is finely minced.

In a small bowl, whisk together the lime juice, fish sauce, red pepper flakes, and erythritol. Set the bowl aside.

Heat the coconut oil in a 10-inch (25-cm) or larger cast iron skillet over medium-high heat. Add the pork mixture and cook it for 6 to 7 minutes, until the pork turns golden brown. Add the green onions and cook for 1 minute.

Pour the sauce over the pork mixture and stir to coat it. Let it caramelize for 1 to 2 minutes. Taste the mixture for salt and add the salt if needed.

Top the pork with the minced mint and cilantro and serve it with the lettuce leaves and cucumber.

# MEATLESS MONDAYS: VEGETARIAN

Keto is too often stereotyped as the bacon and butter diet that's high in animal protein and fats. Sure, you could choose to eat Keto that way, but there are plenty of low-carb, high-fat meatless options to suit any lifestyle. In the next few pages, you'll find delicious vegetarian recipes such as Tomatillo Shakshuka (page 154), Sesame Tofu with Hibachi Zucchini and Onions (page 161), and Cheesy Chile Rellenos (page 162).

## SERVES 4

## NUTRITION

(per serving)

**Calories**
649 kcal

**Fat**
63.4 g

**Protein**
12.1 g

**Carbs**
11.4 g

**Fiber**
5.8 g

**Net Carbs**
5.6 g

# TOMATILLO SHAKSHUKA

**As delicious to eat as it is to say, this tom-ah-tee-yo shack-shoo-kah is a terrific meat-free option for a weekend brunch or a weeknight dinner.**

### Shakshuka
¼ cup (60 ml) avocado oil

½ medium white onion, diced

3 medium jalapeño peppers, minced

4 cloves garlic, minced

1 tsp ground cumin

¼ tsp sea salt

2 cups (500 g) tomatillo salsa

½ cup (30 g) finely chopped fresh cilantro

6 large eggs

### Toppings
⅓ cup (41 g) crumbled Cotija cheese

4 medium radishes, thinly sliced

1 medium jalapeño pepper, thinly sliced

2 medium avocados, thinly sliced

Preheat the oven to 425°F (218°C).

To make the shakshuka, heat the oil in a 10-inch (25-cm) or larger cast iron skillet over medium-high heat. Add the onion, jalapeño peppers, and garlic. Cook the vegetables for 4 to 5 minutes, until they are soft.

Sprinkle in the cumin and salt. Cook the mixture for 30 seconds to toast the spices until they are fragrant. Add the salsa.

Stir in the cilantro and make 6 divots in the mixture. Crack an egg into each one. Transfer the shakshuka to the oven and bake it for 15 minutes, until the egg whites are set but the yolks are still runny.

Top the shakshuka with the Cotija cheese, radishes, jalapeño pepper, and avocados just before serving.

# VEGAN TACO CUPS

*Keto* and *vegan* are two terms that usually don't overlap, but that doesn't mean they can't. These Vegan Taco Cups are loaded with flavor because they utilize seasoned walnuts and cauliflower as the filling. Topped with spicy jalapeño, pico de gallo, and avocado, this is a Meatless Monday meal that the whole family will enjoy.

## SERVES 4

## NUTRITION
(per serving)

**Calories**
490 kcal

**Fat**
45.1 g

**Protein**
8.6 g

**Carbs**
21.9 g

**Fiber**
12.6 g

**Net Carbs**
9.3 g

### Vegan Taco "Meat"
2 cups (214 g) cauliflower florets

1 cup (117 g) walnut pieces

2 chipotle peppers in adobo sauce

1 tbsp (8 g) chili powder

½ tsp ground cumin

½ tsp sea salt

1 tbsp (15 ml) fresh lime juice

3 tbsp (45 ml) avocado oil

### Taco Cups
8 small cabbage leaves

½ cup (120 g) pico de gallo

2 medium avocados, thinly sliced

1 large jalapeño pepper, thinly sliced

4 tbsp (16 g) minced fresh cilantro

To make the vegan taco "meat," combine the cauliflower, walnut pieces, chipotle peppers, chili powder, cumin, salt, and lime juice in a food processor and pulse until the mixture resembles ground beef.

Heat the oil in a 10-inch (25-cm) or larger cast iron skillet over medium heat. Add the "meat" mixture to the skillet and cook it for 5 to 7 minutes, until the cauliflower is soft.

To make the taco cups, divide the "meat" mixture among the cabbage leaves and top the taco cups with the pico de gallo, avocados, jalapeño pepper, and cilantro. Serve immediately.

# BALSAMIC MUSHROOMS
## WITH HERBED VEGETABLE MASH

The Herbed Vegetable Mash with these Balsamic Mushrooms isn't your run-of-the-mill mashed cauliflower. If you can't get enough of this recipe as an entrée, reduce the quantities or double the servings and pair it as a side with your favorite protein.

### Herbed Vegetable Mash

3 tbsp (42 g) unsalted butter

2 cloves garlic, minced

2 tsp (1 g) minced fresh rosemary

2 tsp (1 g) minced fresh oregano

2 tsp (1 g) minced fresh thyme

4 cups (428 g) cauliflower florets

⅔ cup (160 ml) heavy cream

Sea salt, as needed

Black pepper, as needed

1½ cups (75 g) coarsely chopped kale

2 tbsp (30 ml) water

### Balsamic Mushrooms

2 tbsp (30 ml) olive oil

10 oz (280 g) cremini mushrooms

3 tbsp (45 ml) balsamic vinegar

¼ tsp sea salt

¼ tsp black pepper

To make the herbed vegetable mash, heat the butter in a 10-inch (25-cm) or larger cast iron skillet over medium-high heat. Add the garlic, rosemary, oregano, and thyme and cook them for 30 seconds, until they are fragrant. Add the cauliflower and heavy cream. Cover the skillet and simmer the mixture for 15 minutes, until the cauliflower is soft. Transfer the mixture to a food processor and process until it is smooth. If needed, add an additional 1 to 2 tablespoons (15 to 30 ml) of heavy cream to reach your desired consistency. Season the mash with the salt and black pepper.

In the same skillet over medium heat, combine the kale and water. Cover the skillet and cook the kale for 3 to 4 minutes, until it has wilted. Stir the kale into the mashed cauliflower and divide the herbed vegetable mash between four individual serving bowls.

To make the balsamic mushrooms, heat the oil in the same skillet over medium-high heat. Add the mushrooms. Cook the mushrooms for 5 to 7 minutes, until they are soft. Add the vinegar, salt, and black pepper. Cook the mushrooms for 1 to 2 minutes more, until the vinegar has reduced and is thick. Top the herbed vegetable mash with the mushrooms and serve.

# SESAME TOFU
## WITH HIBACHI ZUCCHINI AND ONIONS

The macronutrient profile of tofu is actually very favorable to Keto dieters. In this recipe, the Sesame Tofu truly is the star of the show, but the Hibachi Zucchini and Onions make a strong case for best supporting cast.

**SERVES 2**

**NUTRITION**
(per serving)

**Calories**
424 kcal

**Fat**
35.1 g

**Protein**
23.4 g

**Carbs**
10.3 g

**Fiber**
4.5 g

**Net Carbs**
5.8 g

### Sesame Tofu
1 tbsp (15 ml) sesame oil

8 oz (224 g) firm tofu, diced

2 tbsp (30 ml) low-sodium tamari

2 tbsp (20 g) granulated erythritol

¼ tsp ground ginger

¼ tsp garlic powder

### Hibachi Zucchini and Onions
3 tbsp (42 g) butter

1 medium zucchini, diced

½ cup (80 g) diced onion

Sea salt, as needed

1 tsp sesame seeds

To make the sesame tofu, heat the oil in a 10-inch (25-cm) or larger cast iron skillet over medium-high heat. Add the tofu to the skillet and sear it for 2 to 3 minutes per side, until it is crispy. Add the tamari, granulated erythritol, ginger, and garlic powder. Cook, stirring occasionally, for 2 minutes, until the sauce has reduced. Remove the tofu from the skillet and set it aside. Do not wipe out the skillet.

To make the hibachi zucchini and onions, add the butter, zucchini, and onion to the skillet over medium-high heat. Cook the vegetables for 4 to 5 minutes, until they have softened. Season them with the salt.

To serve, place the sesame tofu on top of the zucchini and onions. Sprinkle each serving with the sesame seeds.

## SERVES 4

## NUTRITION
(per serving)

**Calories**
688 kcal

**Fat**
63.7 g

**Protein**
18.2 g

**Carbs**
13.5 g

**Fiber**
5.9 g

**Net Carbs**
7.6 g

# CHEESY CHILE RELLENOS

We love everything about these Cheesy Chile Rellenos—the gooey, cheesy center encrusted within the charred pepper make every bite a fiesta-worthy moment. The spice level for this meal is quite mild, but if you are sensitive to spicy foods, the poblano pepper is a better bet than the Anaheim pepper.

4 medium Anaheim or Poblano peppers

1½ cups (170 g) shredded Mexican blend cheese

¼ cup (30 g) coconut flour

3 large eggs, whites and yolks divided

1 cup (224 g) refined coconut oil, 1 cup (240 ml) algae oil, or 1 cup (224 g) lard

1 cup (240 ml) low-sugar red enchilada sauce

1 medium avocado, diced or thinly sliced

4 tbsp (48 g) sour cream

1 medium jalapeño pepper, thinly sliced

2 tbsp (8 g) minced fresh cilantro

Using a gas grill, gas burner, or broiler, char the Anaheim peppers for 2 to 3 minutes per side, until they are blistered on each side.

Place the Anaheim peppers in a 10-inch (25-cm) or larger cast iron skillet and cover the skillet with a dish towel for 20 minutes to allow the peppers to steam. Carefully remove as much of the peppers' skins as you can with your hands, then cut a T shape into one side of the peppers, making sure not to cut all the way through. You should have two flaps. Stuff each pepper with one-fourth of the Mexican blend cheese. Close the flaps and set the peppers aside.

Place the coconut flour in a medium bowl and the egg whites in another medium bowl. Using a hand mixer, beat the egg whites for about 2 minutes, until they are light and fluffy. Fold in the egg yolks.

Heat the oil in the same skillet over medium-high heat. Dredge the peppers through the coconut flour, then dip them into the egg mixture. Carefully place the peppers, seam side down, in the oil and fry them for 1 to 2 minutes, until they are brown. Flip the peppers and fry them for 1 to 3 minutes, until they are golden. Set the peppers aside and drain the oil from the skillet.

Add the enchilada sauce to the skillet over medium heat and cook it for 2 to 3 minutes, just until it is hot. To serve, place the sauce on a plate and top it with the peppers. Serve the peppers with the avocado, sour cream, jalapeño pepper, and cilantro.

# ZUCCHINI BOAT PIZZAS

**Zucchini fact: We always think of zucchini as a vegetable, but botanically they are a member of the berry family—so technically, these are fruit pizzas.**

2 medium zucchini, halved lengthwise

2 tbsp (30 ml) olive oil

¼ tsp sea salt

⅛ tsp black pepper

½ cup (120 ml) unsweetened tomato sauce

1 tsp Italian seasoning

1 cup (113 g) shredded mozzarella cheese

2 tbsp (12 g) sliced black olives

2 tbsp (20 g) diced onion

2 tbsp (28 g) diced mushrooms

2 tbsp (28 g) diced bell pepper (any color)

¼ tsp red pepper flakes

Preheat the oven to 350°F (177°C).

Scoop out the middles of the zucchini halves. Place the zucchini halves, cut side up, into a 10-inch (25-cm) or larger cast iron skillet.

Drizzle the zucchini with the oil and season them with the salt and black pepper. Transfer the skillet to the oven and bake the zucchini for about 15 minutes.

In a small bowl, mix together the tomato sauce and Italian seasoning. Once the zucchini are done baking, add the tomato sauce, mozzarella cheese, black olives, onion, mushrooms, bell pepper, and red pepper flakes.

Transfer the skillet to the oven and bake the zucchini until the cheese has melted, 10 to 15 minutes. Serve immediately.

## SERVES 2

## NUTRITION
(per serving)

**Calories**
368 kcal

**Fat**
27.7 g

**Protein**
17.5 g

**Carbs**
15.5 g

**Fiber**
4.2 g

**Net Carbs**
11.3 g

# CHIPOTLE TOFU BOWLS

Tofu is an awesome Keto-friendly option if you tolerate soy well. It's high in fat but still packs a protein punch. Smoky chipotle peppers and a delicious chimichurri "rice" make this bowl super delicious.

**SERVES 4**

**NUTRITION**

(per serving)

**Calories**
492 kcal

**Fat**
39.7 g

**Protein**
22.1 g

**Carbs**
20.7 g

**Fiber**
10 g

**Net Carbs**
10.7 g

### Chipotle Tofu
1 (1-lb [454-g]) block extra-firm sprouted tofu, cut into 1-inch (2.5-cm) cubes

2 tbsp (30 ml) pureed chipotle peppers in adobo sauce

1 tbsp (15 g) tomato paste

1 tbsp (9 g) ground cumin

½ tsp garlic powder

½ tsp onion powder

½ tsp sea salt

3 tbsp (45 ml) avocado oil

### Chimichurri Cauliflower Rice
2 tbsp (30 ml) olive oil

¼ cup (15 g) finely chopped fresh cilantro

1 tbsp (15 ml) fresh lime juice

1 clove garlic

¼ tsp sea salt

4 cups (480 g) cooked cauliflower rice

### Chipotle-Lime Crema
4 oz (112 g) sour cream

Juice of 1 medium lime

½ tsp chipotle powder

Sea salt, as needed

### Bowls
1 medium avocado, diced

¼ cup (120 g) pico de gallo

1 medium jalapeño pepper, thinly sliced

4 medium radishes, thinly sliced

To make the chipotle tofu, in a medium bowl, coat the tofu with the pureed chipotle peppers, tomato paste, cumin, garlic powder, onion powder, and salt. Set the tofu aside.

To make the chimichurri cauliflower rice, combine the olive oil, cilantro, lime juice, garlic, and salt in a food processor and process until the chimichurri sauce is smooth. Set the sauce aside.

To make the chipotle-lime crema, mix together the sour cream, lime juice, chipotle powder, and salt. Refrigerate the chipotle-lime crema until you are ready to serve.

To cook the tofu, heat the avocado oil in a 10-inch (25-cm) or larger cast iron skillet over medium-high heat. Add the tofu in a single layer and cook it for 2 to 3 minutes per side, until it is brown and crispy. Remove the tofu from the skillet and set it aside. Wipe out the skillet.

Add the chimichurri sauce to the same skillet over medium heat. Once the sauce is hot, add the cauliflower rice and cook it for 3 to 4 minutes, until it is soft and fluffy.

To assemble the bowls, divide the cauliflower rice among four individual serving bowls and top each serving with the chipotle tofu, avocado, pico de gallo, jalapeño pepper, and radishes. Drizzle the bowls with chipotle-lime crema and serve.

# WALNUT CHILI

There is nothing better than a warm, hearty bowl of chili when the weather is cool. This vegetarian Walnut Chili is no exception and is a great way to make Meatless Monday your favorite day of the week.

**SERVES 6**

**NUTRITION**
(per serving)

**Calories**
487 kcal

**Fat**
43.9 g

**Protein**
9.4 g

**Carbs**
22.3 g

**Fiber**
11.1 g

**Net Carbs**
11.2 g

## Chili

¼ cup (60 ml) avocado oil

1 medium bell pepper (any color), diced

¾ cup (120 g) diced onion

½ cup (51 g) diced celery

2 medium jalapeño peppers, diced

2 cloves garlic, minced

2 tsp (6 g) chili powder

1 tsp smoked paprika

½ tsp sea salt

1½ cups (176 g) coarsely chopped walnuts

3 tbsp (45 ml) pureed chipotle peppers in adobo sauce

1 (15-oz [450-ml]) can unsweetened tomato sauce

1 (15-oz [420-g]) can fire-roasted diced tomatoes, undrained

1 cup (240 ml) vegetable broth

## Garnishes

2 medium avocados, diced

¼ cup (48 g) sour cream

¼ cup (28 g) shredded Cheddar cheese

4 medium radishes, thinly sliced

2 tbsp (8 g) minced fresh cilantro

To make the chili, heat the oil in a 10-inch (25-cm) or larger cast iron skillet with high sides or a 5-quart (4.8-L) cast iron Dutch oven.

Add the bell pepper, onion, celery, jalapeño peppers, and garlic to the skillet and cook the mixture for 5 minutes, until the vegetables have softened. Stir in the chili powder, smoked paprika, and salt and cook for 1 minute, until the spices are fragrant.

Add the walnuts, pureed chipotle peppers, tomato sauce, diced tomatoes, and broth. Bring the chili to a boil, then reduce the heat to medium-low. Cover the skillet and cook the chili for 30 minutes.

To serve, divide the chili among six individual serving bowls. Garnish each serving with the avocados, sour cream, Cheddar cheese, radishes, and cilantro.

# CLASSIC VEGETABLE SOUP

**This Classic Vegetable Soup takes us right back to being kids, as this was a staple at both of our dinner tables growing up. Sometimes it had beef added to it, but we like this vegetable-only version the best.**

## SERVES 4

## NUTRITION
(per serving)

**Calories**
469 kcal

**Fat**
42.6 g

**Protein**
6.3 g

**Carbs**
20 g

**Fiber**
7.3 g

**Net Carbs**
12.7 g

6 tbsp (90 ml) olive oil

1 small white onion, diced

2 medium bell peppers (any color), diced

3 cloves garlic, minced

1 tbsp (3 g) Italian seasoning

1 small head cauliflower, cut into florets

2 cups (200 g) 2-inch (5-cm) fresh green bean pieces

2 (15-oz [420-g]) cans fire-roasted diced tomatoes, undrained

8 cups (1.9 L) vegetable broth

Sea salt, as needed

Black pepper, as needed

Heat the oil in a 5-quart (4.8-L) cast iron Dutch oven over medium heat. Add the onion, bell peppers, and garlic. Cook the vegetables for 5 to 7 minutes, until they have started to soften.

Add the Italian seasoning and cook the vegetables for 30 seconds, until the Italian seasoning is fragrant.

Add the cauliflower, green beans, diced tomatoes, broth, salt, and black pepper and bring the soup to a boil. Reduce the heat to medium-low. Cover the Dutch oven and cook the soup for 15 minutes.

Taste the soup for salt and adjust the seasoning if necessary. Serve the soup immediately or store it in the refrigerator for up to 4 days or in the freezer for up to 6 weeks.

# ACKNOWLEDGMENTS

### The Cast Iron Keto Blog Readers

We'd like to send a huge thank-you to every single one of our awesome readers, without whom Cast Iron Keto, and thus this book, would not exist. Thank you for your enthusiasm, getting (or at least tolerating) our bad puns and jokes, and always putting a smile on our faces with your lovely comments and emails.

We're thrilled to be able to bring you a book that's filled with easy skillet dinners that are meant to make your lives easier and tastier. Thank you for trusting us with your skillets. We hope you love these recipes as much as we do and that they become staples for you.

### Each Other

To Alex: Thank you, thank you for always being my top supporter, for supporting every crazy idea I've ever had—from starting my first food blog eight years ago to selling all of our belongings so that we could travel the world. Thank you for always washing the dishes and never complaining about having to eat cold food after photoshoots. Thank you for coming on board with me and creating Cast Iron Keto. I'm so lucky to get to create alongside my best friend every single day. I love you.

To Lauren: Thank you! None of this would be possible without you. You are a fantastic photographer, a divine recipe developer, a wonderful wife, and so much more. You constantly amaze me with your ability to take my wild and crazy ideas and somehow turn them into a successful business. You're the best person I know, and you make me a better person just by knowing you. I love our life together, I love our adventures—but most importantly, I love you and don't know where I'd be without you.

### Page Street

To the team at Page Street, thank you all so much for bringing our book to life. Thank you to Marissa, our editor, who believed in the book from the start, and to the design team who took our ideas and made them better than we could have imagined.

# ABOUT THE AUTHORS

**Alex and Lauren Lester** are the creators of the popular food website Cast Iron Keto as well as Healthful Creative, a creative content agency specializing in recipe development and food photography for brands all across the world. Alex and Lauren truly embody Cast Iron Keto's motto of "living an epic life." They spent a year traveling full-time in an RV across the United States, everywhere from the white sands of New Mexico to the coast of Maine and everywhere in between. They now reside in the rainy Pacific Northwest and call Portland, Oregon, home along with their one-eared epileptic cat named Van Gogh and a happy-go-lucky rescue pup named Edison.

# INDEX